3 Doughs

For Alex and Sophie,
May your lives be filled with
adventure, love, friendship
and plenty of good bread.

60 Recipes

3 Doughs

LACEY OSTERMANN

PHOTOGRAPHY BY STEVEN JOYCE

quadrille

60 Recipes

The
Lace
Bakes
Story

Hello, I'm Lacey. I'm originally from Northern California, but now I live in East Sussex in the UK, with my husband, Chris, and our children, Alex and Sophie.

I can't begin to tell you how surprised I am to be writing this book. Five years ago, I didn't even know how to make bread, but 2020 changed everything, sending me off on an unexpected journey full of opportunities. And now here I am, writing a book about bread dough and all the fun and delicious things you can make with it. It's surreal, and quite honestly, it's been an accidental dream come true!

Let me take you back to how it all began ...

It was early 2020 in Hither Green, South East London. My next-door neighbour, Antigone, had been trying to convince me to take a bit of her sourdough starter for months. I felt very intimidated by the idea of baking bread, and our kids were very young – the last thing I needed was something else to take care of and keep alive!

My perspective shifted with the Covid-19 lockdown. I knew we'd be home a lot more, so I finally accepted some sourdough starter, and I followed video tutorials on Instagram – thank you, Sophie (@thescandicook)! – to learn how to make a loaf of sourdough bread.

My bread-iversary – the day I took my first loaf of sourdough out of the oven – was 22 March 2020. I was instantly hooked. It tasted like bread from a bakery. It had a crispy, chewy crust, and a squishy, bubbly interior. I was so proud of it. I look back now with an experienced set of eyes, and I can see that my first loaf was burned, flat and poorly shaped! I didn't care. I had just made my first loaf of bread, and it felt like *magic*.

Stuck at home due to the lockdown, I started making a couple of loaves daily to practise my newfound hobby. My family loved my homemade sourdough, but we couldn't consume the amount of bread I was producing. So I started leaving wrapped loaves on my neighbours' doorsteps and then texting them to open their front door for a surprise!

In those early days of the pandemic, lining up to buy a good loaf of bread from the bakery would take at least 20 minutes. My friend Sophie suggested I should start selling my bread to neighbours so they could avoid these queues, and asked if she and her family could be my first customers. I gauged interest from other neighbours, and there was an overwhelming response: people wanted fresh bread delivered to their doorsteps. I created a WhatsApp group, got my food-safety certificates, and registered with the local council as a home bakery. My friend Heather designed a logo for me and by the end of May, Lace Bakes, my little micro-bakery, was born!

Over the course of 16 months, I sold loaves of sourdough, cookies, cakes, brownies, pizza dough, pancake batter and frozen cookie dough to neighbours and friends. My alarm was perpetually set to 3:45am, and our house was overrun with 25 kg (55 lb) bags of flour from Shipton Mill. You'd find me pushing The BreadBuggy™ (my daughter's pushchair) around the neighbourhood, stacked with crates filled with baked goods to deliver. It was exhausting, but I absolutely loved it. Lace Bakes allowed me to stay connected to my community during a very strange time.

As life got back to normal after the pandemic, our family had social plans again: weekends away, birthday parties, lunches with family and friends. I found it difficult to juggle normal life and the micro-bakery, and it became increasingly clear that it was time to stop selling my bakes. With sadness, I closed Lace Bakes and took a much-needed break.

In early 2022, I started sharing recipes and food videos on social media. A lot of the videos went viral, and my following grew rapidly. I started producing more detailed tutorials, particularly for focaccia and pizza dough, and people seemed to love them. I had no experience in writing recipes, or filming and editing videos, so I just figured everything out as I went.

In early 2023, I started getting interest from a few different publishers. Writing a cookbook hadn't been a goal of mine, but their belief in me and my recipes planted a seed. A couple of days after a chat with the editor of this book, Issy, the concept for *3 Doughs, 60 Recipes* came to me. This collection of recipes feels very authentic and in line with what I already share on social media, but I've also tried to think outside the (bread)box to come up with some exciting and unexpected ways to use the three doughs in this book.

If you've been following my journey for the past few years, I cannot thank you enough. Your continued support has been invaluable to me, and has helped me to shape the concept and content for this book. My hope is that its pages will soon become caked with dough and splattered with olive oil – the true markers of a beloved recipe book. Please continue to tag me in your photos and stories so I can see what you've made, using the hashtag #3doughs60recipes!

If you're new to the Lace Bakes world, I'd like to wish you a very warm welcome. Grab a bag of flour, pop on an apron and let's dough!

Lacey

Introduction

This cookbook is for bread-lovers. Pizza-lovers. Toast-lovers. Sandwich-lovers.

It's for those of you who love to dip and dunk your bread into delicious sauces. For the ones who feel sheer joy at the sight of a cheese pull on a pizza or the sound of a fresh slab of crispy focaccia bread being ripped into. You're safe here. This cookbook encourages all of the above.

It is especially for those of you who have zero experience baking bread. You can make outstanding homemade bread without a stand mixer, a bread machine, a sourdough starter or that special proofing drawer you've probably seen on baking shows. You don't need any of that. (Okay, I do think you should have digital kitchen scales, but we will get to that ...)

What you really need are a few solid dough recipes. Doughs that you will turn to time and time again because they're easy to master, and because you can adapt the way you shape and bake them to achieve the most delicious array of bread creations. You'll also need some go-to recipes for sauces, dips and toppings, which will elevate your enjoyment of bread immensely.

I want to hold your (flour-covered!) hand and show you that, with a few basic concepts under your belt, you can absolutely make bread. I know you can, because I've already taught thousands of beginners how to do it on social media (@_lacebakes_). You might be one of them. If that's the case, hello again, and thank you so much for trusting my recipes enough to buy my cookbook!

Let me show you – like, actually show you – how to make bread. I know that so many of you benefit from watching the bread-making process on video. It really helps to be able to see the correct dough texture, how to do a stretch and fold, or how to knead dough in a simple way. You'll notice that the dough recipe pages contain QR codes for you to scan with your phone. These will direct you to video tutorials that have been crafted to show you, step by step, how to make the three core dough recipes in this book. I'm certain that these visual guides will give you that extra bit of confidence as you embark on your bread-making journey.

For experienced bread-bakers, my hope is that this cookbook will provide you with more go-to dough recipes to add to your established repertoire. I aim to inspire you with ideas for how to enjoy your carby creations, including topping suggestions, exciting new dips, and a few magic tricks to show you how to turn your dough into something completely unexpected. I know there is plenty for you here too.

Right, that's enough talking – let's start baking some bread! First things first: I suggest you have a look at the Bread Basics section (pages 12–14) and the Dough Must-knows section for each core dough. They explain some baking concepts and tips that will be helpful to know before you get started.

Bread Basics
must-know concepts for budding bread-makers

The questions and comments I receive from followers on social media are enormously valuable to me as a recipe developer. They help me understand the typical person's level of knowledge around bread-making, and the common questions that arise when someone is attempting to make bread for the first time. I created this guide to help answer some questions you may have about the bread-making process.

THE IMPORTANCE OF USING DIGITAL SCALES

I'm putting this at the top of the list because I believe it so strongly. I grew up in California, and never had the experience of using digital scales in the kitchen because we measured everything with cups! When I moved to the UK, I learned how to use a digital scale, and I was instantly converted. When I started baking bread, I learned how crucial measurement accuracy is to ensure the flour/water/yeast/salt ratio in the dough is properly balanced. Measurements can, quite honestly, make or break a bread recipe.

You will find metric (grams), imperial (ounce) and cup measurements in this book; this was important to me because I want my recipes to be accessible to everyone. Having said that, I urge you to use digital scales when making the dough recipes. They are inexpensive and very easy to use, and will save lots of mess because you measure straight into the bowl (instead of dirtying up measuring cups). They will ensure your measurements are accurate, which will give you the best chance of success.

If you'd prefer not to acquire digital scales, I do understand. Just be wary of how you measure your flour. I conducted my own experiment and asked five different people to measure a cup of flour. I weighed the contents of each cup, and they yielded five different weights, ranging from 120–160 g (scant 4 oz–5½ oz)! This sort of discrepancy will have an impact on the dough, particularly if you have four or more cups of flour in one batch.

A cup of flour should weigh 125 g (4 oz). The best way to ensure your flour is properly measured without scales is to follow these steps:

1. Fluff the flour with a spoon or fork so it's not compacted in the bag or storage container.
2. Spoon the flour into your measuring cup – do not scoop the cup into the flour, as this will compact the flour and will result in far too much flour per cup!
3. Use the back of a butter knife to level off the flour in your cup before adding the flour to the recipe.

FLOUR & PROTEIN PERCENTAGES

All flours are not created equal. The type of flour you use is enormously important, so be sure to read the 'Dough Must-knows' sections at the start of each chapter to ensure you have the correct flour for the dough you wish to make.

You may notice that I mention using bread flour with a protein content of at least 12 per cent. The protein level is important when it comes to keeping the flour-to-water ratio in the dough in balance, so I wanted to explain how to calculate it in case you find yourself needing to do so. The protein percentage can be found by figuring out how many grams of protein are in 100 g flour. Most bags of flour state that a serving is 30 g, then it will tell you how many grams of protein are in that serving. Let's say there are 4 g of protein per 30 g serving for example.

To calculate the percentage, you first need to divide 100 g by the serving size (30 g): 100 g/30 g = 3.33

Then multiply that number by how many grams of protein are in each serving (4 g) to get the protein content:
3.33 g × 4 g = 13.32 per cent protein

This is all getting a bit technical, and the truth is you don't have to worry too much about calculating this percentage, as most good bread flours will contain more than 12 per cent protein anyway. Some bread flours even list the protein percentage on the label, so you don't need to calculate it at all!

PROOFING & ENVIRONMENTAL TEMPERATURE

You'll notice that each recipe will mention proofing times for the dough. Proofing (also called proving) dough means covering the dough and letting it rest and rise for a period of time. The dough recipes in this book will always be proofed at room temperature, unless you are using the overnight adaptations, which will require proofing overnight in the fridge.

Of course, room temperatures will fluctuate depending on where you live. The timelines stated in this book are based on an environmental temperature of 20°C (68°F), but I don't want you to stress too much about this. All you need to do is consider the temperature of your kitchen – if it's much colder than 20°C (68°F), then the dough will probably need to proof for a bit longer. If it's particularly warm in your kitchen, the yeast will be very active, and the dough will probably need a bit less time to proof.

In each dough recipe, I explain what the dough should look like when it's fully proofed, so on a particularly cold or hot day, use that description as the gauge and adjust the timeline stated in the recipe if you feel you need to so.

'STRETCH & FOLD' VS KNEADING

Why do we need to 'stretch and fold' or knead the dough?

Simply put, the purpose of this action is to help activate the gluten and build its strength in the dough. The stronger the dough is, the more pliable it will become, and it will have a better chance of rising and holding its shape, too. Gluten strength also equates to more bubbles in your dough!

Stretching and folding and kneading achieve the same outcome, but we stretch and fold wetter doughs, and knead drier doughs. If you feel intimidated, don't worry – just scan the QR codes on the dough recipe pages, and I will walk you through how to do each of them in my video tutorials.

YEAST CONVERSIONS

Each of the three dough recipes in this book call for instant yeast (also called fast-action, easy bake or quick-rise yeast). Instant yeast is great because you don't need to activate it before adding it to the dough. You can use other types of yeasts if you prefer, but a few adjustments will be required.

IF YOU'D PREFER TO USE ACTIVE DRY YEAST (ALSO CALLED DRIED ACTIVE YEAST)

Use the same quantity of yeast, but you'll need to activate it first. Whisk together the yeast with the warm water and honey or sugar stated and let it sit for 5–10 minutes, or until the yeast has bloomed – it will look very foamy on the surface when it is ready to use. Add the remaining ingredients and continue the recipe as normal.

IF YOU'D PREFER TO USE FRESH YEAST

Triple the amount of yeast that is called for. If a recipe calls for 4 g (1 teaspoon) instant yeast, then use 12 g (1 tablespoon) fresh yeast.

Activate the fresh yeast as above before adding the rest of the dough ingredients.

YEAST EXPIRY DATES

Yeast will expire and lose its rising power over time. Always make sure the yeast you are using is within its expiry date. Store opened containers of dried yeast in the fridge and use them within 3–4 months. Fresh yeast has a 2–3 week lifespan and must be stored in the fridge.

OVEN SETTINGS & BAKE TIMES

Unless otherwise specified in the recipe, the oven settings quoted in this book are for a conventional (non-fan) electric oven. I love using the fan (convection) setting on my oven, but I realise a lot of people do not have that feature, so I wanted to test the recipes using oven settings that will apply to as many readers as possible.

If you'd like to use a fan oven setting, please ensure that you adjust the baking temperatures stated in the recipes:

- If you measure temperature in Celsius, reduce the stated temperatures by 15–20°C.
- If you measure temperature in Fahrenheit, reduce the stated temperatures by 25–30°F.

I refer to the 'pizza setting' in a few recipes. This is typically a fan setting, so reduce temperatures accordingly if your oven has one and you plan to use it.

The performance of each oven can vary drastically. Never be afraid to add a few minutes to the bake time if the bread looks too pale. It will not overbake if you leave it in for a few extra minutes to achieve the colour you're hoping for! Some ovens just run a little cooler or hotter than others.

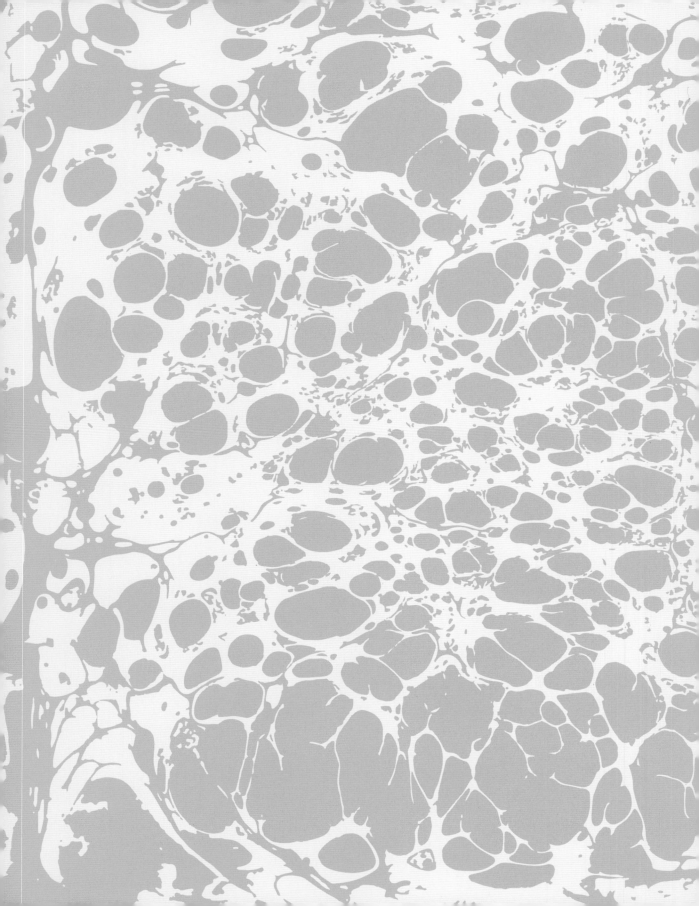

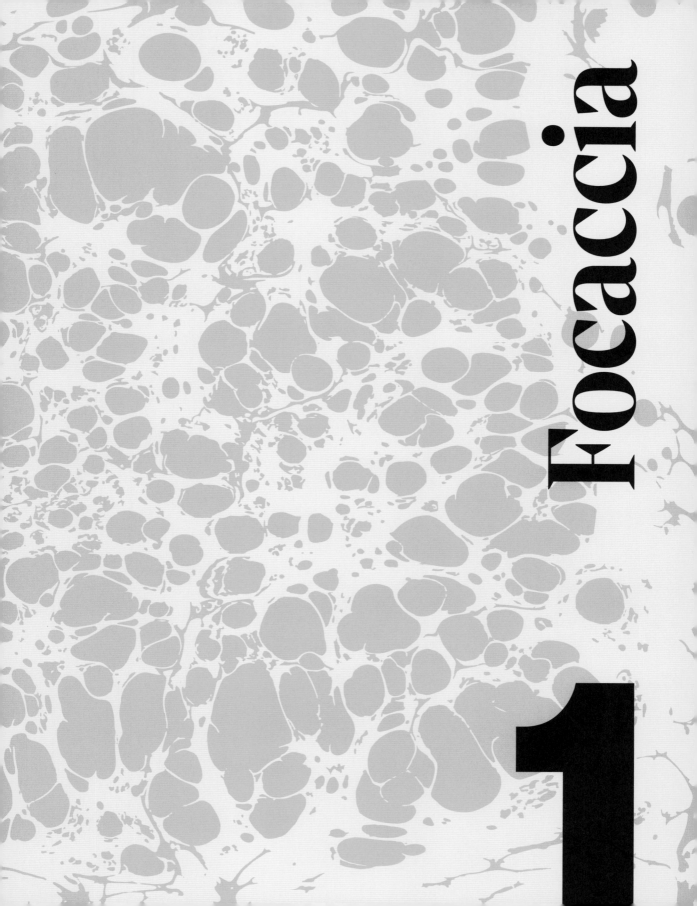

Focaccia

1

There is something magical about *Focaccia*. Dare I say it? She is the Queen of all breads.

This Italian bread is best known for three things: bubbles, olive oil and delicious toppings. The exterior is crispy while the interior remains perfectly soft and squishy, qualities that can be credited to the sheer amount of olive oil and water that the dough contains. It may come as a surprise, but focaccia happens to be one of the easiest breads to make; if you're a bread beginner, this is an excellent place to start.

The most enchanting and satisfying part of the focaccia process is arguably the dimpling. Sinking your fingers into a pillowy tray of dough is a gratifying experience that you can only understand once you've tried it.

Focaccia can be customised to suit the topping preferences of the baker. Savoury or sweet, it can be topped with seasonal vegetables or fruit, and sauces like pesto, fresh herbs, seeds, cheese, or even chocolate if you really have a sweet tooth. I believe that a fresh-from-the-oven slab of focaccia is one of the best things in life, but it doesn't stop there ...

The beauty of focaccia dough is that it can be used in a variety of unexpected ways. I will show you how to rework the dough to turn it into a Roman-style Pizza (page 64), a loaf of Crusty Dutch Oven Bread (page 58), a batch of Soft Sandwich Rolls (page 72), and much more, but first let's check out the Focaccia Dough Must-knows overleaf to ensure you're fully prepared to start working with this dough.

Focaccia Dough
must-knows

STICKY DOUGH

Focaccia dough is wet and sticky.
Dip your hands in water when performing the 'stretch and folds' to help prevent the dough from sticking to your fingers.
Oil your hands when transferring the dough into the tray and when dimpling it.

Take note of the dough in the QR-code video tutorial on page 22 and use it as a gauge for consistency. Every bread flour absorbs different levels of water: if your dough looks wetter, it could just mean your flour absorbs a little less water than mine does. Try reducing the water in the dough by 30 ml (2 tablespoons) next time, and feel free to add a touch more flour to the current batch until the consistency matches that of the dough in the video tutorial.

FLOUR

WHITE BREAD FLOUR

This is the best flour to use for focaccia, because it contains high levels of protein and gluten; these are the building blocks you need to achieve good bubbles in your bread. Aim to use a bread flour with a protein content of at least 12 per cent. See page 13 for how to calculate the protein content of your flour.

PLAIN (ALL-PURPOSE) FLOUR

This type of flour contains less protein and gluten than bread flour. It also can't absorb as much water and you probably won't achieve as many bubbles in your bread. The water in the recipe should be reduced by around 30 ml (2 tablespoons) when using this type of flour. You can then add more if needed to match the consistency of the dough in my video tutorial.

WHOLEWHEAT FLOUR

While wholewheat flour will produce a healthy and flavoursome slab of focaccia, the bread will be denser and less bubbly due to the bran content in the flour. I suggest a mix of 50 per cent wholewheat and 50 per cent white bread flour – and be prepared to add up to an extra 40–50ml (scant–generous 3 tablespoons) of water to the dough.

BAKING TRAY

For baking focaccia, I typically use an aluminium or metal tray measuring at least 23 × 33 cm (9 × 13 in), also known as a quarter sheet pan. If using ceramic or glass, keep in mind that you may need to leave the bread in the oven for a bit longer, and the focaccia may not achieve the same level of crispness.

The size of the baking tray you use will determine the thickness of the focaccia. The 23 × 33 cm (9 × 13 in) baking tray will give you a thicker focaccia. If you'd prefer a thinner, crispier focaccia with more crust, use a larger tray, as the dough will spread out more.

EQUIPMENT

The most important tools for this dough are digital scales and a curved dough scraper. Be prepared to use a lot of extra virgin olive oil and non-stick baking parchment in the focaccia chapter! See page 12 for more on the importance of using digital scales when making bread.

OVEN SETTINGS

OVEN TEMPERATURE

Temperatures stated are for a conventional oven (not fan/convection). See page 14 for how to adjust the temperature for a fan oven.

PLACEMENT OF OVEN RACK

For most ovens, setting the oven rack to the lowest position will help to ensure the bottom of the focaccia gets crispy. One exception is if you have a gas oven with all heat concentrated at the bottom. In this case, bake the focaccia on the middle rack instead.

OVEN SETTINGS

If you have a pizza setting on your oven, always opt to use that for focaccia. This setting directs extra heat to the bottom of the oven, which allows the base of the bread to crisp up while preventing toppings from burning. Be mindful that the pizza setting is often a fan setting, so reduce the temperature as directed on page 14.

BAKE TIMES

If your focaccia still looks pale by the time the suggested bake time has lapsed, leave the bread in the oven until it has reached the colour you're hoping for. If it takes a lot longer than stated, then increase the temperature of your oven by 10–15°C (20–30°F) the next time you make the recipe. After a few attempts and adjustments, you should be able to find the settings that are best for baking focaccia in your oven.

If you're having trouble getting the base crispy, I've found that placing the tray directly on the bottom of the oven for the final 4–5 minutes of baking can help to toast it up nicely!

STORING, FREEZING & REHEATING

Focaccia is always best enjoyed on the day it was baked because the crust will be at its crispiest and the interior at its softest. It can be brought back to its day-one glory by following the steps below.

Wrap any remaining bread tightly in aluminium foil and place it in a large zip-top storage bag. Store it at room temperature for up to 3 days, or in the refrigerator if it has cheese or meat in it, or you can freeze it. If you plan to freeze it, be sure to slice the focaccia into portions before wrapping and freezing so you can simply reheat as many portions as needed.

IF REHEATING FROM ROOM TEMPERATURE

Preheat the oven to 180°C (350°F). Remove the focaccia (still wrapped in foil) from the plastic storage bag and place it in the oven for 10–12 minutes. Peel back the foil and bake for an additional 2–3 minutes to ensure the crust crisps up.

IF REHEATING FROM FROZEN

Preheat the oven to 200°C (400°F). Remove the focaccia (still wrapped in foil) from the plastic storage bag and place it in the oven for about 15 minutes, then peel back the foil and bake for an additional 2–3 minutes so the crust crisps up.

Same-day Focaccia

MAKES 1 SLAB OF FOCACCIA (12 SERVINGS)

TIME: 3–3¾ HOURS, DEPENDING ON PROOFING TIMES

420 ml (14¼ fl oz/1¾ cups) warm water at 40–43°C (105–110°F)

6 g (1½ teaspoons) instant yeast*

5 g (1 teaspoon) honey, sugar or agave

60 ml (4 tablespoons/¼ cup) extra virgin olive oil, plus extra for drizzling

500 g (1 lb 2 oz/4 cups) white bread flour

10 g (2 teaspoons) fine sea salt

toppings of your choice

flaky sea salt, for sprinkling

*if you are using active dry or fresh yeast, please refer to page 14

stage 1

Mix, Stretch & Fold, & First Proof

1. In a large mixing bowl, whisk together the warm water, instant yeast, honey and 15 ml (1 tablespoon) of the extra virgin olive oil until everything has dissolved. Add the bread flour and salt, and mix very well with a spoon until no dry patches of flour remain. Cover the bowl with a clean tea towel and leave the dough to proof for 15 minutes at room temperature.

2. After 15 minutes, it is time to stretch and fold. Dip your hand into a bowl of water before touching the dough to prevent it from sticking to your fingers. Now take hold of the edge of the dough at the 12 o'clock position. Pull it up to stretch, then pull it down over the bulk of the dough, finishing in the 6 o'clock position. Repeat this action on all sides of the bowl until the dough has tightened up. If the dough doesn't tighten up into a ball, don't worry! The main point here is that you have stretched the dough to develop the gluten strength.

3. Cover the bowl and leave to proof for another 15 minutes, then stretch and fold once more. You may notice it's easier to stretch the second time around – this is because the gluten in the dough has started to develop.

4. Gather your dough into a rough ball shape and position it in the bowl smooth-side up. Cover the bowl and leave to proof, undisturbed, for about 1–1½ hours at room temperature. The dough should have nearly doubled in size and should be puffy, bubbly and jiggly. (See page 13 for more on proofing times and how to adjust for warm/cold temperatures.)

Scan the QR code for a video tutorial to accompany the recipe!

stage 2

Preparing the Tray & Second Proofing

5. To prepare the tray (see page 20 for tray size guidance), rub a tiny bit of the remaining olive oil onto it, then place a sheet of non-stick baking parchment on top and press down. The oil will help the parchment to stay in place. Now drizzle the remaining 45 ml (3 tablespoons) of olive oil onto the baking parchment, spreading it evenly around the base and sides. The non-stick parchment prevents the focaccia from sticking to the tray when baking, while still allowing the bread to crisp up at the bottom.

6. Using a curved dough scraper or an oiled hand, gently release the dough from the sides of the bowl and tip it on to the oiled baking tray.

7. Oil your hands and fold one side of the dough towards the middle. Repeat with the other side, folding it over the top as if you are folding a piece of paper into thirds (it will look like a large burrito). Rotate the dough so its long side aligns with the long side of the tray, then flip it over so the seams from the folding are at the bottom and the top is smooth.

8. Cover the tray to prevent the dough from drying out and forming a crust as it proofs. You can use another (inverted) baking tray for this, or an oiled piece of baking parchment, but do not use cling film (plastic wrap) or a tea towel, as these will stick.

9. Proof at room temperature for about 1–1½ hours. Exact proofing times will depend on the temperature. If it's a hot day, it might only take 1 hour for the dough to puff up and spread, but on a very cold day, it could take 2 hours. While the dough is proofing, prepare any toppings you plan to dimple into your focaccia.

Dimple, Top & Bake

10. When the dough is ready, it should be puffy, bubbly and jiggly, and it will have spread out to mostly fill the space in the tray. If it hasn't spread out completely, oil your hands, slide them under the dough and gently pull the dough towards the edges until it fills the tray and is a uniform thickness. If you're using a larger tray, you may not need to stretch it all the way to the edges.

11. Preheat the oven to 220°C (430°F) and move the oven rack to the lowest position. (See page 21 for more on oven settings for focaccia.)

12. Drizzle the top of the dough with 15–30 ml (1–2 tablespoons) extra virgin olive oil, then oil your hands. Using both hands, press your fingers into the dough, gently touching them to the bottom of the tray. Repeat until the entire tray of dough is dimpled.

13. Top with a sprinkle of flaky sea salt, then press any extra toppings firmly into the little dimples you've created.

14. Bake the focaccia for 18–25 minutes, or longer if needed, until it is a golden-brown colour.

15. Once it's out of the oven, allow the focaccia to cool for a couple of minutes in the baking tray, then transfer to a cooling rack so the bottom of the bread remains crispy.

16. You can finish the focaccia with an extra drizzle of extra virgin olive oil at this point if you wish for it to look burnished and glistening. Let it cool for at least 15–20 minutes before you slice (or tear) and enjoy! See page 21 for instructions on storing, freezing and reheating focaccia.

Make it Ahead – Overnight Focaccia

Making three adjustments to the recipe will allow you to make the dough a day or two before you plan to bake it.

- Use less yeast: Instead of 6 g (1½ teaspoons) instant yeast, use 4 g (1 teaspoon) when mixing the dough. The yeast is reduced because the dough will be fermenting for a longer period of time.
- Refrigerate overnight: Instead of letting the dough rest at room temperature for 1–1½ hours after the second stretch and fold, drizzle the top of the dough with a little bit of extra virgin olive oil and cover the bowl tightly with a lid or plastic wrap, then place in the refrigerator overnight.
- Allow more time for proofing before baking: The next day, follow the instructions on page 24 for transferring the dough to the baking tray, but allow at least 2 hours for it to proof at room temperature before baking. It will need a little more proofing time than the same-day version because the dough will be very cold after being removed from the fridge. Follow the remaining steps as normal.

See Focaccia Dough Must-knows on page 21 for instructions on storing, freezing and reheating focaccia.

The Classic:
Rosemary & Sea Salt

This is arguably the most popular focaccia topping, and for very good reason –
IT JUST TASTES SO GOOD. This focaccia provides a neutral base for sandwiches,
and it is probably the 'safest' focaccia to bring along as a gift for a friend!

**MAKES 1 SLAB
OF FOCACCIA
(12 SERVINGS)**

1 batch of Same-day Focaccia
dough (page 22)
3–4 fresh rosemary sprigs
15–30 ml (1–2 tablespoons)
extra virgin olive oil, for
drizzling
flaky sea salt, for sprinkling

1. Prepare the Same-day Focaccia dough up to step 10 on page 27.
2. Rub the rosemary sprigs with a little extra virgin olive oil; this will help to prevent the leaves from burning in the oven. Remove the rosemary leaves from the stems and roughly chop half of them, leaving a few pretty clusters of leaves intact.
3. Preheat the oven to 220°C (430°F) and move the oven rack to the lowest position.
4. Drizzle the focaccia dough with the extra virgin olive oil, then scatter the chopped rosemary evenly over the top of the dough. Rub a little olive oil onto your fingers, then dimple the tray of focaccia, pushing the chopped rosemary into the dough. Gently push the rosemary leaf clusters into the dimples, spacing them out as artfully as possible.
5. Sprinkle generously with flaky sea salt, then bake for 18–25 minutes, or longer if needed, until golden brown. Allow to cool for a couple of minutes in the baking tray, then transfer to a cooling rack for at least 15–20 minutes before serving.

TOPPING TIP:

If you're a fan of olives, push
some pitted olives into the
dough after dimpling. I like
to cut some in half and leave
the others whole, as I think
a variation makes for a very
pretty focaccia.

Jalapeño Cheddar Focaccia

My brother Austin loves this focaccia. He will remind me months before I visit him in California that I need to bake it as soon as I arrive. And I don't blame him: studded with spicy pickled jalapeños and pockets of savoury Cheddar, this is probably one of my favourites, too!

MAKES 1 SLAB OF FOCACCIA (12 SERVINGS)

1 batch Same-day Focaccia dough (page 22)

15–30 ml (1–2 tablespoons) extra virgin olive oil, for drizzling

200 g (7 oz) Cheddar, half cut into small cubes and half grated

1–2 handfuls of pickled jalapeños, drained and patted dry

flaky sea salt, for sprinkling

1. Prepare the Same-day Focaccia dough up to step 10 on page 27. While the dough is proofing in the tray, prepare the toppings.
2. Preheat the oven to 220°C (430°F) and move the oven rack to the lowest position.
3. Once the dough has fully proofed, drizzle with the extra virgin olive oil and dimple with your fingers. Press the cubes of cheese and the jalapeños into the dimples you've created. Sprinkle some flaky sea salt over the top.
4. Bake for 15 minutes, then remove the focaccia from the oven and scatter the grated cheese evenly over the top. Return to the oven and bake for an additional 10–12 minutes until the cheese is starting to crisp up.
5. Allow to cool for a couple of minutes in the baking tray, then transfer to a cooling rack and wait at least 15 minutes before slicing and serving.

TOPPING TIP:

You can use fresh jalapeños if you prefer; just make sure to coat the slices in a little bit of extra virgin olive oil before using to prevent them from burning. And if you are baking for someone who can't quite handle the heat, leave off the jalapeños altogether and follow this method to make a cheesy focaccia.

Garlic Butter & Cheese-stuffed Focaccia

You may notice that I've included a version of cheesy garlic bread for each of the doughs in this book. Why? Social media tells me that the people want their cheesy garlic bread! Every time I post this flavour combo, the internet goes wild. Once you tear into this bread and see the oozy, garlicky cheese inside, you'll understand why.

**MAKES 1 SLAB
OF FOCACCIA
(12 SERVINGS)**

1 batch of Same-day
 Focaccia dough (page 22)
15–30 ml (1–2 tablespoons)
 extra virgin olive oil, for
 drizzling
210 g (7½ oz/generous
 2 cups) grated mozzarella
2 tablespoons Parmesan
 or vegetarian Italian-style
 hard cheese, finely grated

FOR THE GARLIC BUTTER

30 g (2 tablespoons) salted
 butter
30 ml (2 tablespoons) extra
 virgin olive oil
10 garlic cloves, minced
2 tablespoons freshly
 chopped flat-leaf parsley
flaky sea salt (optional)

TOPPING TIP:

Serve alongside a bowl of
warm Perfect Pizza Sauce
(page 161) for dipping, or
use the focaccia to make
chicken Parmesan or
meatball sandwiches.

1. Prepare the Same-day Focaccia dough up to the end of step 4 on page 22 (before you tip it into the oiled tray). Prepare the baking tray as instructed on page 24, step 5.
2. To make the garlic butter, melt the butter with the extra virgin olive oil in a small frying pan over a medium–low heat. Add the garlic and reduce the heat to low. Simmer for 1–2 minutes, then add the parsley, along with a pinch of salt if you feel it's needed. Set aside to cool slightly.
3. Tip the dough into the oiled baking tray and gently spread it out towards the edges of the tray so there is plenty of surface area to accommodate the garlic butter and cheese.
4. Scoop most of the solid garlic and parsley bits out of the butter mix and scatter them evenly over the top of the dough, along with about two-thirds of the melted butter and oil. Reserve the rest for brushing over the top after the focaccia has been baked.
5. Sprinkle half of the grated mozzarella on top of the garlic butter. Oil your hands and fold one side of the dough towards the middle. Repeat with the other side, folding it over the top of the folded dough. Rotate the dough so its long side aligns with the long side of the tray, then flip it over so the seams are at the bottom. The garlic and cheese should be nicely encased in the dough while it proofs.
6. Cover with an inverted baking tray or a piece of oiled baking parchment, and proof at room temperature for 1–1½ hours.
7. Preheat the oven to 220°C (430°F) and move the oven rack to the lowest position.
8. Drizzle the top of the dough with the extra virgin olive oil and dimple the focaccia with your fingers. Bake for 15 minutes, then remove from the oven and evenly sprinkle the remaining mozzarella over the top. Bake for another 8–10 minutes, or until the cheese is a light golden brown.
9. Remove from the oven and brush the remaining garlic butter over the top, then finish with a sprinkle of finely grated Parmesan. Allow to cool for a couple of minutes in the tray, then transfer to a cooling rack for at least 15 minutes before slicing and serving.

Chimichurri Focaccia

Chimichurri is a flavour-packed, oil-based condiment that is commonly used in both Argentinian and Uruguayan cuisines. Dimpling chimichurri into focaccia is by no means traditional, but I'm happy to break the rules when it tastes this good. Fun fact – the video I posted for this in 2022 was my first mega-viral video, with over 33 million views!

MAKES 1 SLAB OF FOCACCIA (12 SERVINGS)

1 batch Same-day Focaccia (page 22)
1 batch Chimichurri Sauce (see below)
flaky sea salt, for sprinkling

1. Prepare the Same-day Focaccia dough up to step 10 on page 27. While the dough is proofing in the tray, make the chimichurri sauce (see below).
2. Preheat the oven to 220°C (430°F) and move the oven rack to the lowest position.
3. When the focaccia has finished proofing in the tray, give the chimichurri sauce a good stir, then drizzle about 3 tablespoons of it over the dough. Dimple the chimichurri into the focaccia using your fingers, then sprinkle over the flaky sea salt.
4. Bake for 20–25 minutes until golden brown. Remove from the oven and brush with more chimichurri sauce.
5. Allow to cool for a couple of minutes in the baking tray, then transfer the focaccia to a cooling rack for at least 15 minutes before serving. There will be some chimichurri sauce left over; this makes for an incredible dipping oil to enjoy with the bread.

Chimichurri Sauce

MAKES 240 G (8½ OZ/1 CUP)

30 g (1 oz/½ cup) finely chopped flat-leaf parsley
30 g (1 oz/½ cup) finely chopped coriander (cilantro)
1 teaspoon dried oregano
3 garlic cloves, minced
1 red chilli, deseeded and finely diced
30 ml (2 tablespoons) red wine vinegar
120 ml (4 fl oz/½ cup) extra virgin olive oil
1 teaspoon flaky sea salt
freshly ground black pepper, to taste

1. In a medium-sized bowl, stir together all the ingredients. Taste and adjust the seasoning if needed.
2. Cover and leave the flavours to marinate for at least 20 minutes before serving. You can make this in advance and store it for up to 3 days in a sealed container in the fridge.

TOPPING TIP:

Check out page 49 for ideas on how use the chimichurri sauce on a Focaccia Slab Sandwich, or try it on my Roasted Pepper & Chimichurri Pizza (page 156).

Loaded Baked Potato Focaccia

Potatoes on bread? YES. This one is dedicated to the carb-lovers. Here, a slab of focaccia is jam-packed with all the delicious things that make loaded baked potatoes so good. Potatoes. Cheese. Bacon. Chives. Need I say more?

MAKES 1 SLAB OF FOCACCIA (12 SERVINGS)

1 batch Same-day Focaccia dough (page 22)

1 medium-sized baking potato

8 rashers smoked streaky bacon

15–30 ml (1–2 tablespoons) extra virgin olive oil, for drizzling

175 g (6 oz/1¾ cup) Cheddar, grated

4 spring onions (scallions), finely diced

8 chives, finely chopped, to garnish

flaky sea salt, for sprinkling

1. Prepare the Same-day Focaccia dough up to step 10 on page 27. While it is proofing in the tray, start prepping the toppings.
2. Thinly slice the potato using a sharp knife or mandoline. Place the potato slices into a bowl filled with cold water and let them sit for at least 15 minutes.
3. Cook the bacon in a frying pan over a medium heat, but don't make it quite as crispy as you normally like it, as it will continue cooking in the oven later. Chop it into small bite-sized pieces.
4. Preheat the oven to 220°C (430°F) and move the oven rack to the lowest position.
5. Once the focaccia dough has fully proofed, remove the potatoes from the water and pat them dry with kitchen paper. Coat the potatoes with a thin layer of extra virgin olive oil.
6. Drizzle the focaccia with the olive oil, then evenly scatter two-thirds of the cheese over the top of the dough, along with half the bacon and half the spring onions. Using your fingers, dimple these toppings into the dough.
7. Arrange the potato slices in a single layer over the top, then sprinkle with flaky sea salt.
8. Bake the focaccia for 15 minutes, then remove from the oven and sprinkle with the remaining cheese, bacon and spring onions. Return to the oven and bake for another 10–12 minutes until the potatoes and cheese are beginning to crisp up.
9. Sprinkle the chives over the top. Allow the focaccia to cool in the tray for a couple of minutes, then transfer to a cooling rack and wait at least 15 minutes before serving.

TOPPING TIP:

Sliced potatoes also work brilliantly with the Rosemary & Sea Salt Focaccia on page 30. Use the potato-soaking method above: the water removes some of the starch from the potatoes, which allows them to crisp up more as they bake.

Pear, Walnut & Rosemary Focaccia

If you think fruit doesn't belong on top of a focaccia, think again. I love to serve fruit-and-nut focaccia alongside a cheeseboard, with honey for drizzling. It is unbelievably delicious. This recipe was inspired by my dear friend and cookbook author Anna Ansari. She sent me a photo of her son helping her make this using my dough recipe, and I knew I had to try it for myself!

MAKES 1 SLAB OF FOCACCIA (12 SERVINGS)

1 batch Same-day Focaccia (page 22)
100 g (3½ oz/1 cup) walnuts, roughly chopped
1 large ripe pear (or 2 small)
2 rosemary sprigs
15–30 ml (1–2 tablespoons) extra virgin olive oil, for drizzling
flaky sea salt, for sprinkling

TOPPING TIP:

If you like, you can add a few additional walnuts to the top of the focaccia, but be mindful that they may get a little extra toasted during the baking process. Stuffing most of them into the dough helps to ensure they won't burn.

MORE FRUIT-AND-NUT TOPPING COMBOS TO TRY ...

- cherry & almond
- peach & pistachio
- fig & walnut
- plum & hazelnut
- strawberry & pistachio
- apple & pecan
- grape & walnut
- blueberry, lemon & almond

1. Prepare the Same-day Focaccia dough up to the end of step 6 on page 24.
2. Once the dough is in the oiled baking tray, gently spread it out so there is plenty of surface area to sprinkle the walnuts onto. Scatter the nuts over the top of the dough, then oil your hands and fold one side of the dough towards the middle. Repeat with the other side, folding it over the top of the folded dough. Rotate the dough so its long side aligns with the long side of the tray, then flip it over so the seams are at the bottom. Cover and proof at room temperature for 1–1½ hours.
3. Preheat the oven to 220°C (430°F) and move the oven rack to the lowest position.
4. While the oven is preheating, core and thinly slice the pears. Remove the rosemary leaves from their stems and coat them in a little extra virgin olive oil.
5. When the focaccia has finished proofing in the tray, drizzle it with the extra virgin olive oil, then use your fingers to dimple the dough. Gently push the pear slices into the dough and nestle the rosemary needles into some of the dimples you've created.
6. Drizzle with extra virgin olive oil once more, then sprinkle over some flaky sea salt. Bake for 18–22 minutes, or until the focaccia is golden brown.
7. Allow to cool for a couple of minutes in the baking tray, then transfer to a cooling rack for at least 15 minutes before serving.

Hot Chocolate Focaccia

This squidgy focaccia is swirled with sweet hot chocolate mix, studded with chocolate chips and dimpled with salted butter and coarse sugar. Unsurprisingly, it's a favourite among children and chocolate-lovers alike!

MAKES 1 SLAB OF FOCACCIA (12 SERVINGS)

1 batch of Same-day Focaccia dough (page 22)
75 g (5 tablespoons) hot chocolate powder mix
165 g (5¾ oz/1 cup) chocolate chips
15 ml (1 tablespoon) extra virgin olive oil
1½ tablespoons salted butter, melted
2 tablespoons Demerara (turbinado) sugar

1. Mix the Same-day Focaccia dough as instructed on page 22. Then, before the first stretch and fold, evenly sprinkle 1 tablespoon of the hot chocolate powder and a third of the chocolate chips over the dough. Perform the stretch and fold as normal (page 22, step 2), then cover the bowl and leave to proof for 15 minutes.
2. Now sprinkle another tablespoon of the chocolate powder and another third of the chocolate chips over the dough and perform a second stretch and fold to incorporate the chocolate into the dough. Cover the bowl once more and proof for about 1–1½ hours.
3. Line the baking tray with non-stick baking parchment, and evenly spread the extra virgin olive oil all over the parchment. Tip the dough into the tray and gently spread it out so there is plenty of surface area. Sprinkle the remaining 3 tablespoons of chocolate powder over the dough, then oil your hands and fold one side of the dough towards the middle. Repeat with the other side, folding it over the top of the folded dough. Rotate the dough so its long side aligns with the long side of the tray, then flip it over so the seams are at the bottom. Cover and proof at room temperature for 1–1½ hours.
4. Preheat the oven to 215°C (420°F) and move the oven rack to the lowest position.
5. Evenly drizzle the melted butter over the top of the dough, then sprinkle over the sugar and remaining chocolate chips. Dimple the dough using your fingers, then bake for 18–22 minutes, or until the focaccia is golden brown.
6. Allow to cool in the baking tray for a couple of minutes, then transfer to a cooling rack and wait at least 20 minutes before serving.

THINK OUTSIDE THE (BREAD)BOX:

Use leftover slices of this bread to make the Focaccia French Toast on page 56.

Mini Focaccia Rounds

Why settle on one focaccia flavour when you can try up to eight flavours using only one batch of dough? My kids love helping with these, because they get to choose their own toppings. These are the ideal size for sandwiches, and they also pair well with a crunchy summer salad or a comforting bowl of soup.

MAKES 8 FOCACCIA ROUNDS

1 batch Same-day Focaccia dough (page 22)
15–30 ml (1–2 tablespoons) extra virgin olive oil, for drizzling
toppings of your choice (see below)
flaky sea salt, for sprinkling

MINI FOCACCIA FLAVOUR IDEAS

- jalapeños & Cheddar
- Fresh Basil Pesto (page 155), mozzarella & cherry tomatoes
- bacon, Cheddar & spring onions
- Everything Bagel Seasoning (page 93)
- rosemary & sea salt
- potatoes & rosemary
- Perfect Pizza Sauce (page 161), mozzarella & basil
- chocolate chips
- seasonal fruit, nuts & herbs
- cinnamon sugar

1. Prepare the Same-day Focaccia dough up to the end of step 4 on page 22. After the dough has fully proofed in the bowl, continue with the recipe here.
2. Line two large baking trays (each about 33 × 46 cm/13 × 18 in) with non-stick baking parchment and coat the paper with extra virgin olive oil.
3. Rub some extra virgin olive oil onto your work surface and tip the dough onto it. Using an oiled dough scraper or sharp knife, divide the dough into eight portions, each weighing around 118 g (scant 4 oz).
4. Shape each portion into a dough ball by gently pulling each side of the blob of dough towards the middle and then pinching it so it is secured into a ball shape. Flip each dough ball over so the seams are on the bottom, and place on the prepared trays. There should be four dough balls on each tray, spaced well apart.
5. Cover the dough and proof at room temperature for 45 minutes. It's a bit tricky to cover these unless you have another large tray to invert over the top. Instead, I usually measure out two more pieces of non-stick baking parchment and rub excess oil from the baking trays/ worktop onto them before draping the oiled side over the dough.
6. Prepare your toppings of choice while the dough balls proof, and preheat the oven to 215°C (420°F) with the oven racks set to the middle and bottom positions.
7. Drizzle some more olive oil over the top of the dough balls, then use your fingers to thoroughly dimple each mini focaccia. If using cheese, sprinkle it over the top of the focaccia before dimpling it in. If using a sauce like pesto, spread it over the dough before dimpling it in. Nestle any big toppings like cherry tomatoes, olives or jalapeños into the dimples. Sprinkle with flaky sea salt.
8. Bake for 14–16 minutes, swapping the baking trays after 8 minutes so they all bake evenly.
9. Remove from the oven and transfer to a cooling rack so the bottoms stay crispy. Allow to cool for at least 10 minutes before enjoying.

Focaccia Slab Sandwiches

Focaccia slab sandwiches are a great time-saving solution when you need to feed a crowd. I've served these at birthday parties, school fundraisers, barbecues and casual gatherings in our home, and they are always a huge hit! Below, you'll find inspiration for a few different slab sandwich flavours, and a formula to help you plan for ingredient quantities.

SERVES 8 FOR LUNCH, 16 FOR AN APPETISER

1 slab of Focaccia
toppings of your choice
(see below)

Slab sandwich formula

1. **Bake** a slab of focaccia in the flavour of your choice. Once the bread has cooled, slice it horizontally down the middle.
2. **Spread** the interior of the bread with the condiment or sauce of your choice. Plan for roughly 200 g (7 oz/¾ cup) sauce, spread evenly across both sides of the bread.
3. **Fill** by topping the bottom side of the bread with the meat, cheese, vegetables and greens of your choice. Plan for roughly 750 g–1 kg (1 lb 10 oz–2 lb 4 oz) of fillings, spread evenly across the bread. If you want to heat your sandwich and you're using fresh salad ingredients, don't add them yet.
4. **Heat** (optional) by placing the focaccia halves on a baking tray (open-faced). Preheat the oven to 180°C (350°F), then bake for 12–15 minutes, or until the cheese has melted and the bread is starting to crisp up. Remove from the oven and add any fresh salad ingredients.
5. **Cut** by squishing the top and bottom of the slab sandwich together and slicing to your desired size. One slab will yield 8 decent-sized sandwiches or up to 16 mini sandwiches. Secure each portion with a toothpick and place on a pretty platter to serve.

Flavour inspiration

PESTO CAPRESE ⓥ
To spread: Fresh Basil Pesto (page 155) or store-bought pesto.
To fill: Fresh mozzarella or burrata, large slices of tomato, fresh basil leaves and rocket (arugula) salad. Drizzle the salad with extra virgin olive oil and aged balsamic vinegar, and finish with a sprinkle of freshly grated Parmesan. Grilled chicken is a great addition here, if you like.

CHIMICHURRI ⓥ
To spread: Chimichurri Sauce (page 36).
To fill: Grilled steak, chicken or slices of fresh mozzarella, along with plenty of sautéed peppers and onions (sauté in a bit of the chimichurri sauce).

HAM & CHEESE
To spread: Dijonaise (two parts mayonnaise and one part Dijon mustard, stirred to combine).
To fill: Thinly sliced deli ham and the sliced cheese of your choice. Add lettuce, tomatoes, pickles or onions if desired. This sandwich can be served hot or cold.

TURKEY, BACON & AVOCADO
To spread: Homemade Ranch Dressing (page 96).
To fill: Thinly sliced deli turkey, crispy smoked bacon, shredded iceberg lettuce, sliced tomatoes and ripe avocado (3 large avocados). Season the avocados and tomatoes with salt and pepper. This sandwich can be served hot or cold. If serving hot, I recommend adding some sliced cheese.

Barbecue Chicken & Bacon Focaccia Stack

Focaccia makes the perfect base for any sandwich you can dream up. This one is stacked high with grilled chicken, barbecue sauce, crispy bacon, melted cheese and crunchy slaw. Serve with a pile of napkins – she's a messy one!

MAKES 1 LARGE SANDWICH (SERVES 1–2)

FOR THE SANDWICH
13 × 13 cm (5 × 5 in) slab of focaccia, sliced horizontally
70 g (2¼ oz/¼ cup) smoky barbecue sauce, plus extra to serve
3 slices Monterey Jack or Cheddar
1 chicken breast (about 185 g/6½ oz)
¼ teaspoon garlic granules
¼ teaspoon paprika
¼ teaspoon flaky sea salt
10 twists of freshly ground black pepper
1 teaspoon extra virgin olive oil
4 rashers smoked streaky bacon
1 tablespoon crispy fried onions (optional)

FOR THE SLAW
100 g (3½ oz/1 cup) white cabbage, finely shredded
40 g (1½ oz/¼ cup) carrot, grated
1 spring onion, finely diced
3 tablespoons Homemade Ranch Dressing (page 96) or store-bought ranch dressing, plus extra to serve
1½ teaspoons seasoned rice wine vinegar
flaky sea salt (optional)

1. Preheat the oven to 180°C (350°F).
2. First, prepare the slaw so the cabbage has a bit of time to soften up. In a bowl, toss together the cabbage, carrots, spring onion, ranch dressing and seasoned rice vinegar. Taste for seasoning and add a pinch of flaky sea salt if needed. Set aside.
3. Place the two halves of the focaccia on a baking tray and spread the cut sides of the bread with the barbecue sauce. Arrange the sliced cheese on the cut side of the half that will be the top part of the sandwich. Bake for 10–12 minutes.
4. While the bread is in the oven, heat a large frying pan over a medium–high heat. Pound the chicken breast with a meat tenderiser or rolling pin until it is an even thickness. In a small bowl, mix the garlic granules with the paprika, salt, pepper and extra virgin olive oil, then spread this evenly on both sides of the chicken.
5. Place the chicken and the bacon into the hot frying pan. Cook the chicken for about 3–4 minutes on each side, or until it is cooked through (the internal temperature should be 74°C/165°F). Cook the bacon to your liking, turning it when needed and removing from the pan once it's reached your desired level of crispiness.
6. Remove the focaccia halves from the oven and arrange the bacon rashers on top of the cheese. Pile the slaw onto the bottom half of the focaccia, then slice the chicken and place on top. Drizzle the chicken with a little more ranch dressing and barbecue sauce, and sprinkle over the crispy fried onions, if using. Top with the top focaccia half, squish both sides of the sandwich together, then slice in half and enjoy.

Daddy O's Focaccia Breakfast Sandwich

Focaccia is the perfect canvas for a variety of sandwiches, but I particularly love using it for breakfast sandwiches. I first made this sandwich as a special treat for my husband Chris on Father's Day, and it instantly became a household favourite.

MAKES 1 LARGE BREAKFAST SANDWICH

½ medium avocado, sliced
2 large slices tomato
4 rashers smoked streaky bacon
10 × 13 cm (4 × 5 in) slab of focaccia, sliced horizontally
extra virgin olive oil, for cooking
1 large egg
2 tablespoons Fresh Basil Pesto (page 155) or store-bought pesto
flaky sea salt and freshly ground black pepper

1. Season the avocado and tomato slices with salt and pepper, then set aside.
2. In a large frying pan over a medium–high heat, cook the bacon until it has reached your desired level of crispiness. Set aside.
3. Wipe away most of the rendered bacon fat from the frying pan, then reduce the heat to medium and place the focaccia halves in the pan, cut-sides down, to toast for 2 minutes, then flip to toast on the other side for another minute.
4. While the focaccia is toasting, drizzle a little oil into a small frying pan over a medium–high heat. Once the oil is hot, crack the egg into the pan, then reduce the heat to medium. Add a small splash of water to the pan to create steam to cook the egg, then immediately cover it with a lid (or a plate if you don't have a lid to fit). After about 2 minutes or once the egg white is completely set but the yolk is still runny, remove the lid from the frying pan and season the egg with salt and pepper.
5. Remove the toasted focaccia from the large frying pan and spread the cut sides with the pesto. Place the tomato slices on the bottom half, followed by the crispy bacon and avocado, then transfer the egg on top. Top with the top half of the focaccia and enjoy!

Focaccia Panzanella Salad with Burrata

Panzanella salad is a great way to use up leftover odds and ends of focaccia. Bake the bread into croutons and then mix with a vibrant array of crunchy veggies, zingy dressing and lots of fresh basil. Top it all off with a ball of creamy burrata cheese, and you've got yourself an easy summertime meal that is guaranteed to impress your guests. After all, it is bread masquerading as salad – who doesn't love that?

SERVES 4

FOR THE CROUTONS
350 g (12 oz) staling focaccia, cut into 2.5 cm (1 in) cubes
2 tablespoons extra virgin olive oil
flaky sea salt and freshly ground black pepper

FOR THE SALAD
350 g (12 oz) cherry tomatoes, halved
1 teaspoon flaky sea salt
½ cucumber, halved lengthways, deseeded and very thinly sliced
½ batch of Pink Pickled Onions (page 96) or 1 small red onion, thinly sliced
1 red (bell) pepper, chopped
20 fresh basil leaves, sliced, plus extra to serve

FOR THE DRESSING
100 ml (3½ fl oz/scant ½ cup) extra virgin olive oil, plus extra to serve
2 tablespoons balsamic vinegar
1 tablespoon red wine vinegar
1 garlic clove, finely minced
1 small shallot, finely chopped
1 teaspoon honey or agave
½ teaspoon Dijon mustard

TO ASSEMBLE
150 g (5 oz) burrata or dollops of Stracciatella (page 70)

1. To make the croutons, preheat the oven to 190°C (375°F). Scatter the focaccia cubes on a large baking tray. Drizzle with extra virgin olive oil and sprinkle with a little salt and pepper, then massage the oil and seasonings into the focaccia cubes. Bake for 15 minutes, or until the croutons are crispy on the outside with a little softness inside.

2. Meanwhile, tip the halved cherry tomatoes into a large bowl and season them with 1 teaspoon flaky sea salt and some black pepper. Set aside for 10 minutes.

3. In a medium bowl, whisk together the dressing ingredients. After the salted tomatoes have rested for 10 minutes, give them a little squeeze to help them release their juices, then drain, reserving the juices. Tip the salted tomato juice and any squeezed-out seeds into the dressing bowl and whisk again. Check the seasoning and adjust if needed.

4. In a large bowl, combine the drained tomatoes with the cucumber, onions and red pepper. Add the basil and croutons, then pour over the dressing and toss everything together well. Check the seasoning and adjust to taste.

5. Serve on a platter or in a pretty bowl, topped with torn pieces of burrata (or dollops of stracciatella). Drizzle the burrata with extra virgin olive oil, then finish with a final sprinkle of salt and pepper and some more sliced basil leaves.

Focaccia French Toast

I particularly love using focaccia for French toast, because the bubbles in the bread act as a safe and cosy place for all the melted butter and maple syrup to nestle into. If you have leftover Hot Chocolate Focaccia (page 44) or a fruit focaccia (page 40), this is a delicious way to use up a few spare slices. You can also use plain focaccia here – just add a little more sugar and cinnamon to the egg mixture.

SERVES 2

2 eggs
2 tablespoons milk
½ teaspoon granulated sugar
¼ teaspoon ground cinnamon
¼ teaspoon pure vanilla
  extract
3 slices sweet focaccia,
  roughly 2.5 cm (1 in) thick
1 tablespoon salted butter,
  for frying, plus extra to
  serve
icing (confectioner's) sugar,
  for dusting
warm maple syrup, to serve

1. Whisk together the eggs, milk, sugar, cinnamon and vanilla in a rectangular dish that is large enough to accommodate the focaccia slices. If you're not using a sweet focaccia to make this, add an extra ½ teaspoon of sugar and a little more cinnamon.
2. Place a large frying pan over a medium heat to start heating.
3. Lay the focaccia slices into the dish and press them down into the egg mixture. Allow them to soak up the egg for about a minute, then flip them over to absorb the egg on the other side.
4. Add the butter to the frying pan and let it melt, brushing it over the entire surface. Place the soaked focaccia slices into the pan and reduce the heat to medium–low. Cook for about 3 minutes on each side.
5. Transfer the Focaccia French Toast to a plate and top with a pat of salted butter. Dust liberally with icing sugar, then drizzle over as much warm maple syrup as you desire.

TOPPING TIP:

Try adding some fresh seasonal fruit to the top of your Focaccia French Toast for a real brunchtime treat!

Easy Dutch Oven Bread

Imagine the kind of loaf you'd find in a bakery: one with a crispy, chewy crust and a soft, squishy interior. Guess what? You can make a bakery-style loaf of bread using focaccia dough at home – the secret is baking it in a Dutch oven (casserole dish). You'll need a Dutch oven (cast-iron casserole dish/pot) measuring at least 4.7 litres (5 quarts).

MAKES 1 LARGE LOAF

1 batch Same-day Focaccia
  dough (page 22)
plain (all-purpose) flour, for
  dusting

1. Prepare the Same-day Focaccia dough up to the end of step 4 on page 22. If you've made this recipe before and have noticed the dough is particularly wet, reduce the water quantity by 30 ml (2 tablespoons). Some bread flours absorb less water than others, and while this doesn't matter as much when baking focaccia, shaping this loaf can be a little tricker if the dough is super wet.

2. Once the dough has finished proofing for 1–1½ hours in the bowl, place your casserole dish into the oven and preheat to 250°C (480°F). If your oven doesn't reach this temperature, set it as high as it goes.

3. Now it's time to shape the loaf. (There are images on the next page to give you a visual guide.) Even if you have reduced the water quantity, the dough will still be very sticky and wet, so flour is your friend here. Liberally dust your work surface with flour, then tip the dough onto the floured surface. Flour your fingers and, using both hands, take hold of the top edge of the dough. Pull it up to stretch, then pull it down over the rest of the dough, about two-thirds of the way towards the bottom. Now take the bottom edge of the bread and pull it up and over the portion of dough you just pulled down. Repeat this pulling-over motion with the right and left sides. When you've finished, the dough should have tightened up into a ball-like shape. Remember, you can flour your fingers between each pulling motion to help prevent sticking.

4. Flip the dough ball upside down so the smooth side is at the top. Dust a little flour over the dough, then cup your hands around it and slowly start pulling it around in a slow, circular shape. You'll notice that the ball of dough will tighten up and start to look smoother around the edges. Repeat this motion until the dough ball feels slightly taut. This shaping step is important for creating tension in the dough, which will help your bread to rise nicely.

5. Measure out a piece of non-stick baking parchment big enough for the dough to sit in the middle with about 7.5 cm (3 in) of extra space on either side. This will create 'handles' you can use while lowering the bread into the preheated Dutch oven.

6. Place the dough in the middle of the piece of baking parchment, then cover with an inverted bowl and leave to proof for 30 minutes while the oven continues to preheat.

7. After 30 minutes, it's time to score the bread. While you can try to use a bread lame (a razor with a wooden holder), I find that a sharp serrated knife does a good job here. No fancy equipment needed!

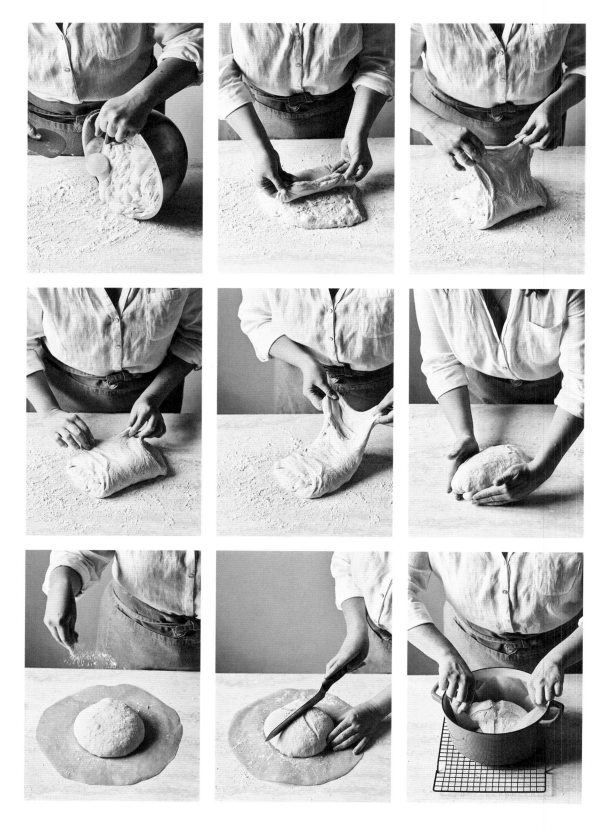

With a quick and decisive swipe, make a cut about 1 cm (½ in) deep into the dough, scoring it all the way across. If you'd like, you can make another score in the opposite direction, but one score will be enough. Scoring the dough encourages it to expand in a controlled way as it bakes. Without scoring, the bread will expand and burst in sporadic places, and may not rise as much as you would like it to.

8. Using heavy-duty oven gloves, remove the preheated pot from the oven and place it on a heatproof surface, then remove the lid and set it to the side. Carefully lift the bread using the baking parchment 'handles' and lower the bread into the pot. Place the lid back on and return the pot to the oven. Set a timer for 38 minutes.

9. After 38 minutes, remove the lid to check on the colour of the bread. It should be a deep golden-brown, and it should sound hollow when you tap the bottom. Replace the lid if you think it needs a few more minutes. My oven typically takes 40–43 minutes, but this could vary depending on the strength of your oven.

10. Once the bread has finished baking, remove the pot from the oven using heavy-duty oven gloves, then transfer to a cooling rack. It's best to allow the loaf to cool for at least 30–45 minutes before slicing, as slicing it too soon can release a lot of steam and negatively affect the texture of the bread. For storage, freezing and reheating, see 'Sandwich Bread Dough Must-knows' on page 80.

What if I don't have a Dutch oven or cast-iron casserole dish?

You can still bake this bread without a casserole dish, but you will need to reduce the oven temperature and add a source of steam to the oven so that the bread can rise to its full potential.

Place a loaf tin filled with hot water at the bottom of the oven while it preheats to 230°C (450°F). Place the dough on a baking tray lined with baking parchment and bake for 25 minutes, then remove the tin of water from the oven and reduce the temperature to 210°C (410°F) and bake for a further 12–16 minutes.

THINK OUTSIDE THE (BREAD)BOX:

Slices of this bread can be used for any of the toast or sandwich recipes you'll find in the Sandwich Bread chapter. It's particularly good for the California BLT (page 96) or the Pesto Chicken Melt (page 98). Don't forget to try it with some of my Homemade Butter (page 101), too!

Cinnamon Raisin Bread

The smell of this bread alone is worth trying this recipe for! The combination of warming cinnamon and plump raisins is truly hard to beat. My son, Alex, who HATES raisins, LOVES this bread, and has proclaimed that he could eat it every day for the rest of his life. High praise. It uses the same baking technique as the Easy Dutch Oven Bread on page 58, so you'll need a Dutch oven (cast-iron casserole dish/pot) measuring at least 4.7 litres (5 quarts).

MAKES 1 LARGE LOAF

1 batch of Same-day
   Focaccia dough, water
   reduced by 30 ml
   (2 tablespoons) (page 22)
140g (scant 5 oz/1 cup)
   raisins
dash of vanilla extract
7 g (1½ tablespoons) ground
   cinnamon
plain (all-purpose) flour, for
   dusting

1. Mix the Same-day Focaccia dough according to the instructions on page 22, step 1, but reduce the water by 30 ml (2 tablespoons) to account for the additional moisture the soaked raisins will add to the dough.
2. Just after mixing the dough, place the raisins into a small bowl. Add the vanilla extract, then pour over enough boiling water to cover. Let the raisins soak for at least 10 minutes, then drain and squeeze the raisins to remove any excess water. Tip the drained raisins into a bowl and stir in the cinnamon until they're evenly coated.
3. Once the dough has been resting for 15 minutes, it is time to stretch and fold. Sprinkle half of the cinnamon-coated raisins over the top of the dough, then wet your fingers to prevent sticking, and take hold of the edge of the dough at the 12 o'clock position. Pull it up to stretch, then pull it down over the bulk of the dough, finishing in the 6 o'clock position. Repeat this action on all sides of the bowl until the dough has tightened up. Cover the bowl and let the dough rest for 15 minutes.
4. After 15 minutes, scatter the rest of the raisins over the dough and repeat the stretch-and-fold process. Cover the dough and let rest for 1–1½ hours at room temperature.
5. Now follow steps 2–10 on pages 58–61 (Easy Dutch Oven Bread) to bake your loaf.

TOPPING TIP:

You can use this folding method to add other inclusions to your loaves, such as olives, seeds, herbs, cheese or even chocolate chips. Remember to remove excess moisture from wet inclusions like olives or pickled jalapeños by blotting them dry before folding them into the dough.

Roman-style Pizza Bases

Also known as *pizza alla pala*, Roman-style pizza is hands down the most beloved street food in Rome. Loaded with beautifully fresh toppings, these rectangular flatbread pizzas are a great way to showcase seasonal produce.

MAKES 2 LARGE ROMAN-STYLE PIZZA BASES (EACH BASE SERVES 2)

1 batch of Same-day
  Focaccia dough (page 22)
fine semolina, for dusting
extra virgin olive oil
toppings of your choice
  (see tip)

1. Prepare the Same-day Focaccia Dough up to the end of step 4 on page 22.
2. While the dough is proofing in the bowl, line a 33 × 46 cm (13 × 18 in) baking tray with non-stick baking parchment and sprinkle it with a little fine semolina, then set aside.
3. Once the dough has finished proofing in the bowl, sprinkle your work surface liberally with fine semolina – do not skimp on this! The countertop should be covered (not dusted!) with fine semolina. Tip the dough onto the work surface and sprinkle more semolina over the top. Using a dough scraper or sharp knife, cut the dough in half, then gently shift the pieces of dough so the seams from the cut are underneath and each piece is a lengthened oval shape. Place them a few inches away from each other, then cover with a clean tea towel and leave to proof for at least 30 minutes, or up to 1 hour.
4. Near the end of the proofing time, preheat the oven to 240°C (465°F), or as high as it can go if it doesn't reach that temperature, and move the oven rack to the lowest position. If your oven has a pizza setting, use that but adjust the temperature as advised on page 14.
5. Carefully transfer one of the pieces of dough to the prepared tray – a large dough scraper will make it easier to lift/transfer the dough. Leave the other piece to continue proofing while you bake this.
6. Using your fingers, dimple the dough thoroughly. After dimpling, slide your hands under the dough and gently stretch it out until it is a long, rectangular shape (around 25 × 40 cm/10 × 16 in). The dough should be quite thin.
7. Drizzle with extra virgin olive oil and bake for 10 minutes, or until it's just starting to brown on top, then remove the pizza base from the oven. Top with your desired sauce, cheese and toppings, then continue baking for an additional 8–12 minutes, or until the crust is golden and the cheese is completely melted.
8. Remove from the oven and add any fresh toppings you're using. Freshly grated Parmesan, a drizzle of garlic oil, fresh basil leaves, dollops of fresh pesto, burrata or prosciutto are all best added after the pizza has been removed from the oven.
9. Transfer the pizza to a cooling rack to ensure the base stays crispy. Cut it lengthways down the middle, then make 2–3 cuts in the opposite direction to create large slices. Repeat with the remaining dough to make a second pizza.

TOPPING TIP:

For some topping inspiration, check out the Lemony Artichoke Roman-style Pizza (page 69) and the Prosciutto and Homemade Stracciatella Roman-style Pizza (page 70).

Lemony Artichoke Roman-style Pizza

Full of bright, fresh, zesty flavours, this is the dreamiest pizza to serve during the summer months when al fresco dining reigns.

MAKES 1 ROMAN-STYLE PIZZA (SERVES 2)

1 Roman-style Pizza Base, unbaked (page 64)
extra virgin olive oil, for drizzling
175 g (6 oz/1¼ cups) grated mozzarella
1 batch Lemony Artichoke Tapenade (see below)

FOR THE ROCKET SALAD

25 g (1 oz/1 cup) rocket (arugula) leaves
1 tablespoon freshly grated Parmesan or vegetarian Italian-style hard cheese, plus extra to serve
2 teaspoons extra virgin olive oil
squeeze of lemon juice
flaky sea salt and freshly ground black pepper

TOPPING TIP:

This tapenade makes a great addition to a grilled cheese sandwich, or you could serve it on crostini for a bruschetta appetiser.

1. Prepare the Roman-style Pizza Base up to the end of step 6 on page 64. Note that you will only need one pizza base for this recipe.
2. Preheat the oven to 240°C (465°F), or as high as it will go if it doesn't reach that temperature, and move the oven rack to the lowest position.
3. Drizzle the pizza base with extra virgin olive oil and bake for 10 minutes, then remove from the oven and scatter the grated mozzarella over the bread. Dot the tapenade evenly over the cheese and then spread it out in an even layer.
4. Return the pizza to the oven for another 8–12 minutes. While it's baking, assemble the rocket salad by tossing together the ingredients in a medium-sized bowl.
5. When the pizza crust is golden brown and the artichoke topping is heated through, remove from the oven and transfer to a cooling rack to ensure the base stays crispy. Scatter the rocket salad over the top, then garnish with more freshly grated Parmesan before slicing into squares to serve.

Lemony Artichoke Tapenade

MAKES 390 G (14 OZ/ 1½ CUPS)

400 g (14 oz) tin or jar artichoke hearts in brine, drained
4 tablespoons extra virgin olive oil
1 teaspoon lemon zest
1½ teaspoons lemon juice
2 garlic cloves, minced
10 g (½ oz) fresh basil, finely chopped
20 g (¾ oz/4 tablespoons) Parmesan, grated
½ teaspoon flaky sea salt
freshly ground pepper

1. Squeeze any excess water from the artichoke hearts, then chop them very finely.
2. Transfer to a bowl, then add the extra virgin olive oil, lemon zest, lemon juice, minced garlic, chopped fresh basil, Parmesan, salt and pepper. Mix everything together, then taste and adjust the seasoning if needed.

Prosciutto & Homemade Stracciatella Roman–style Pizza

Some of you may be asking ... what is stracciatella? If you're familiar with burrata, stracciatella is the rich and creamy filling you find encased inside the outer shell of the cheese. You can easily make your own stracciatella at home, and I'll show you how to in this recipe. Here, the homemade stracciatella is paired with tomato sauce, prosciutto, fresh basil and extra virgin olive oil to create a memorably decadent pizza.

MAKES 1 ROMAN-STYLE PIZZA (SERVES 2)

1 Roman-style Pizza Base, unbaked (page 64)
extra virgin olive oil, for drizzling
300 g (10½ oz/1¼ cups) One-minute Pizza Sauce (page 144) or Perfect Pizza Sauce (page 161)
20 fresh basil leaves
1 batch of Homemade Stracciatella (see below)
90 g (3¼ oz) sliced prosciutto
freshly grated Parmesan, to serve

1. Prepare the Roman-style Pizza Base up to the end of step 6 on page 64. Note that you will only need one pizza base for this recipe.
2. Preheat the oven to 240°C (465°F) and move the oven rack to the lowest position.
3. Drizzle the pizza base with extra virgin olive oil and bake for 10 minutes, then remove from the oven and spread the pizza sauce over the base. Tear 10 of the fresh basil leaves in half and scatter them over the pizza sauce. Drizzle the base with some more extra virgin olive oil, then return to the oven to bake for an additional 8–10 minutes, or until the base is golden brown around the edges.
4. Remove from the oven and transfer to a cooling rack to ensure the base stays crispy. Spread the stracciatella over the entire surface, then lay the prosciutto slices over the top of the cheese. Garnish with the remaining basil leaves, a drizzle of extra virgin olive oil and some freshly grated Parmesan. Slice and serve.

Homemade Stracciatella

MAKES 200 G (7 OZ)

125 g (4 oz) ball fresh mozzarella
4½ tablespoons double (heavy) cream
⅛–¼ teaspoon flaky sea salt (adjust to your preference)

1. Tear the mozzarella ball into tiny shreds, then place in a bowl.
2. Add the cream and ⅛ teaspoon flaky sea salt, then stir until well combined. Taste and add more salt if you feel it needs it – some brands of fresh mozzarella are saltier than others, so adjust accordingly.

TOPPING TIP:

This homemade stracciatella can be used as a burrata substitute in any of the recipes in this cookbook. Burrata can sometimes be costly or difficult to find, but thankfully a similar taste and texture can be achieved with stracciatella.

Soft Sandwich Rolls

I really should have called these 'Magic Sandwich Rolls' – one moment you have a bowl of jiggly focaccia dough, the next moment you've turned the dough into soft and squishy rolls, perfect for cramming all your favourite sandwich fillings into.

MAKES 6 LARGE ROLLS

1 batch Same-day Focaccia dough (page 22)
plain (all-purpose) flour, for dusting

THINK OUTSIDE THE (BREAD)BOX:

These rolls are an ideal base for tomato bruschetta. Slice them down the middle, brush with olive oil or garlic butter, and bake at 180°C (350°F) until the bread is nicely toasted. Top with Marinated Tomatoes (page 148) and cut to desired size.

1. Prepare the Same-day Focaccia dough up to the end of step 4 on page 22. If you've made this recipe before and have noticed the dough is particularly wet, reduce the water quantity by 30 ml (2 tablespoons). Some bread flours absorb less water than others, and while this doesn't matter as much when baking focaccia, it can make handling these rolls a little tricky.

2. Line a 33 × 46 cm (13 × 18 in) tray with non-stick baking parchment. Scatter flour liberally over the parchment and set aside.

3. When the dough has finished proofing in the bowl, liberally dust your work surface with flour and tip the dough onto it. Generously sprinkle some flour over the top of the dough, then gently pull the sides of the dough outwards until it forms a rough rectangle. Carefully pat down any thicker areas in the middle so you're left with a mostly even layer of dough.

4. Using the edge of a large dough scraper or a sharp knife, mark out the indentations for the bread rolls. You can cut the dough into any size you'd like; for example, one batch will make 3 long baguette-shaped rolls, 6 generously sized sub sandwich rolls, or 10–12 small dinner rolls.

5. Cut through the indentations and separate the individual pieces of dough from one another. Place them on the prepared baking tray, spaced well apart, then cover with a clean tea towel and leave to proof for 45 minutes.

6. Near the end of the proofing time, preheat the oven to 240°C (465°F), or as hot as it will go if it doesn't reach this temperature, and move the oven rack to the lowest position. Half-fill a 13 × 23 cm (9 × 5 in) loaf tin with hot water and place it at the very bottom of the oven while it preheats. This will help to create a steamy environment for your rolls.

7. Transfer the rolls to the oven and bake for 12 minutes, then carefully remove the pan of water and continue baking the rolls for another 10–14 minutes, or until the rolls are a deep golden brown. Smaller rolls will take less time, larger rolls will take more time.

8. Remove from the oven and transfer to a cooling rack. Let the rolls cool for at least 10 minutes before serving. These rolls can be stored in a large zip-top storage bag for up to 3 days at room temperature. To freeze, place them in a large freezer bag and take them out individually as needed. To reheat, bake from frozen at 200°C (400°F) for 6–10 minutes or until the bread is thawed and heated through.

Super Seeded Brötchen

One thing I learned after I married into my husband's German family: Germans are serious about good bread. During family visits to the Hamburg area, I noticed that it is normal to make a special trip to the *Bäckerei* to gather fresh bread rolls (*Brötchen*) each morning before breakfast. I remember being so impressed by this unwavering dedication to fresh bread. For the full German breakfast experience, try serving some fresh Brötchen alongside an array of thinly sliced ham, salami, cheeses, boiled eggs, jam, honey, chocolate spread and butter.

MAKES 9 ROLLS

1 batch Same-day Focaccia
  dough (page 22)
plain (all-purpose) flour,
  for dusting
200 g (7 oz/1⅓ cup) mixed
  seeds (I use pumpkin,
  sesame, flax and
  sunflower)

TOPPING TIP:

Replace the mixed seeds
with Everything Bagel
Seasoning (page 93), or
stick to using one type
of seed, like sesame or
pumpkin seeds.

1. Prepare the Same-day Focaccia dough up to the end of step 4 on page 22. If you've made this recipe before and have noticed the dough is particularly wet, reduce the water quantity by 30 ml (2 tablespoons). Some bread flours absorb less water than others, and while this doesn't matter as much when baking focaccia, it can make handling these rolls a little tricky.

2. Line a 33 × 46 cm (13 × 18 in) tray with non-stick baking parchment. Scatter flour liberally over the parchment and set aside.

3. When the dough has finished proofing in the bowl, spread 100 g (3½ oz) of your mixed seeds on the work surface in a rectangular shape measuring roughly 25 × 25 cm (10 × 10 in). Tip the dough onto the seeds and use your hands to spread out the dough, ensuring that the bottom of the dough is covered in seeds. Sprinkle the remaining seeds evenly over all areas of exposed dough, pressing them into the top and sides.

4. Using a dough scraper or sharp knife, cut the dough into three equal strips, then cut each of those strips into three equal-sized pieces. It doesn't matter if they're perfectly uniform in shape.

5. Transfer the Brötchen to the prepared tray. Press any excess seeds from the worktop into the areas of the dough where the cuts were made. Cover with a clean tea towel and leave to proof at room temperature for 45 minutes.

6. Near the end of the proofing time, preheat the oven to 240°C (465°F), or as hot as it will go if it doesn't reach this temperature, and move the oven rack to the lowest position. Half-fill a 13 × 23 cm (9 × 5 in) loaf tin with hot water and place it at the very bottom of the oven while it preheats. This will help to create a steamy environment for your rolls.

7. Transfer the rolls to the oven and bake for 12 minutes, then carefully remove the pan of water and continue baking the rolls for another 10–14 minutes, or until the rolls are a deep golden brown. Smaller rolls will take less time, larger rolls will take more time.

8. Remove from the oven and transfer to a cooling rack. Let the rolls cool for at least 10 minutes before serving. They can be stored in a large zip-top storage bag for up to 3 days at room temperature. To freeze, place in a large freezer bag. To reheat, bake from frozen at 200°C (400°F) for 6–10 minutes or until thawed and heated through.

Sandwich Bread

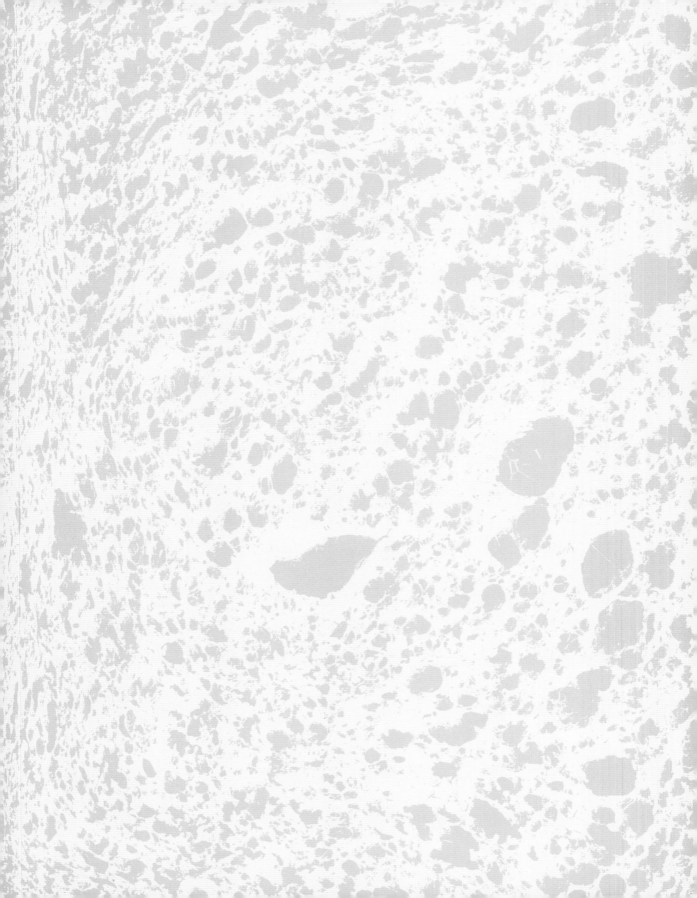

Have you ever heard that phrase people use when describing something great? 'It's the best thing since *sliced bread*!'

When I hear it, I can't help but think, what's so great about sliced bread? The sliced bread I think of is wrapped in plastic bags and stacked in rows on supermarket shelves. Often, it's full of ingredients I can't pronounce. It is flimsy and full of air – there is really nothing to bite into! That's not great, is it?

I think it's time we make sliced sandwich bread that really is the best thing.

This chapter will be centred around a dough that contains ingredients you will recognise. It creates a loaf of sandwich bread that is fluffy yet sturdy: the type of bread you turn to when you need a couple of slices to make a simple sandwich or some buttery toast. But is that all you can use this dough for? Absolutely not. In fact, this is probably the most versatile of the three doughs in this book ...

I'll show you how to turn sandwich bread dough into Brilliant Bagels (page 118), Cinnamon Caramel Monkey Bread (page 126), Giant Soft Pretzels (page 112), Cheesy Garlic Swirls (page 116), Burger Buns (page 122) and more! But first, check out the 'Dough Must-knows' on page 80 to ensure you're fully prepared to start working with this dough.

Sandwich Bread Dough
must-knows

FLOUR

Bread flour with around 12 per cent protein achieves the best results for sandwich bread, but plain (all-purpose) flour will still make a decent loaf. If using plain flour, hold back 30 ml (2 tablespoons) of the water at the beginning, and add it gradually if you feel the dough needs it to come together. The dough should feel a bit tacky, but not overly sticky. I find that the bread rises and holds its shape better when using bread flour.

Unless stated in the recipe, do not add flour to the work surface when working with this dough, as it can really dry out the final product. Instead, lightly coat your work surface with a tiny bit of neutral-tasting oil to help prevent the dough from sticking, if you feel it is necessary.

KNEADING

If you're a bread newbie and feel intimidated by kneading, I'm hoping the that the Sandwich Bread video tutorial (see QR code on page 82) will demonstrate that it doesn't need to be difficult. There really is no right or wrong way to knead bread dough; you just need to ensure you're working the gluten in the dough in one way or another.

EQUIPMENT

If you have a stand mixer, or a handheld mixer with dough hooks, you can save time and effort by using it to knead your dough. To make sandwich bread, you'll need a 900 g (2 lb) loaf tin (usually measuring 23 × 13 cm/9 × 5 in), and if you'd like to make the monkey bread on page 126, you'll need a Bundt tin. As always, I recommend you use a digital scale to measure your ingredients when making the dough – see page 12 for more on this.

STORING, FREEZING & REHEATING

Sandwich bread is best used within 3 days of baking. Store the loaf in a large zip-top plastic bag or wrap it in an extra-large beeswax wrap. If you'd like to freeze this bread, slice the loaf first and then place the slices into a large freezer bag. Remove as much air as possible from the bag before sealing. You can remove slices from the bag and thaw them, or toast from frozen as needed. If you prefer, you can freeze an entire loaf of sandwich bread. Wrap the loaf tightly in foil, then place in a large freezer bag. Remove excess air from the bag before placing in the freezer. To reheat, remove the loaf from the bag and place it in an oven heated to 180°C (350°F), still wrapped in the foil, for 25 minutes, or until heated through.

Sandwich Bread Dough

MAKES 1 LOAF, 12 SLICES

stage 1

**TIME: 3–3¼ HOURS,
DEPENDING ON
PROOFING TIMES**

80 ml (2¾ fl oz/generous
5 tablespoons) whole or
semi-skimmed milk, plus
extra for brushing

30 g (1 oz/2 tablespoons)
salted butter, cut into
small cubes, plus extra for
greasing the tin

225 ml (8 fl oz/scant 1 cup)
warm water (40–43°C/
105–110°F)

12 g (1 tablespoon) instant yeast*

15 g (1 tablespoon) honey,
granulated sugar or
agave syrup

500 g (1 lb 2 oz/4 cups)
white bread flour

8 g (1¼ teaspoons) fine sea salt

neutral-tasting oil or softened
butter, for oiling the bowl

*if you are using active dry or
fresh yeast, please refer to
page 14

Scan the QR code
for a video tutorial to
accompany the recipe!

Mix & Kneading

1. To ensure the liquid components of the recipe are at the perfect temperature, place the milk and butter into a small bowl and microwave for about 45 seconds. If you don't have a microwave, you can combine the milk and butter in a small saucepan and gently warm until the butter has just melted. Stir until the butter has completely melted into the milk, then pour into a large mixing bowl or the bowl of a stand mixer.

2. Pour in the warm water and stir to combine. The mixture should be around 38–43°C (100–110°F). You can check this with a digital thermometer if you wish, or just go by touch – it should feel warm but not hot.

3. Add the instant yeast and honey, and whisk until no lumps of yeast remain.

4. Tip the bread flour into the bowl, then scatter the fine sea salt over the top of the flour. Mix all the ingredients together with a spoon, or mix using the dough hook attachment of a stand mixer until all the flour is incorporated into the dough and no dry patches remain. The dough will look quite shaggy.

5. You have a few options for kneading, depending on the equipment available to you. No matter the method you use, the dough should feel smooth, elastic and slightly tacky (but not sticky) after the kneading is complete.

Kneading with stand mixer:
Continue mixing on a medium speed with a dough hook for about 7–8 minutes.

Kneading with handheld mixer:
Attach the dough hook attachment to your handheld mixer. Place the dough hook(s) into the premixed dough, then turn the mixer on to a medium speed. Knead the dough for 7–8 minutes.

Kneading by hand:

Place the dough on a clean work surface (no flour) and work it into a large ball. Knead it using your favourite method. If you don't have a favourite method, you can use my preferred method: use the heels of your palms to firmly push the dough away from you, then pull the dough back towards you again. Repeat this motion until the dough lengthens into a log-like shape; when this happens, form it back into a ball and repeat the process for 8–10 minutes. It may feel sticky at first, but avoid adding flour, as it can negatively impact the consistency of the bread. To see a video of me demonstrating this kneading method, scan the QR code on page 82.

stage 2

First Proof & Shape

6. Remove the dough from the mixing bowl and lightly grease the bowl with a neutral-tasting oil or softened butter. Tuck the edges of the dough beneath itself to form a large dough ball with a smooth top, then return it to the bowl and cover with a clean tea towel. Leave it to proof at room temperature for about an hour. After this time, the dough should have risen to about double its original size, though it's worth noting that the exact time this will take can be dependent on the temperature of your environment – see page 13.

7. When the dough has finished rising, prepare a non-stick 900 g (2 lb) loaf tin by generously greasing the interior with softened butter.

8. Tip the dough onto a clean work surface and remove the air by patting it down into a rectangle. It should be about 25 × 35 cm (10 × 14 in). Fold in both shorter ends of the rectangle so they meet in the middle of the dough. Starting from the shorter end, roll the dough as tightly as possible into a cylindrical shape. For a more tidy looking loaf, you can pinch together the edges of the dough (where the swirl from rolling is). Place the dough, seam-side down, into the prepared loaf tin. If the cylinder of dough is slightly longer than the length of the tin, simply tuck the ends under the rest of the dough as you place it in the tin.

stage 3

Second Proof & Shape

9. Cover the tin with a clean tea towel or some cling film (plastic wrap) and leave to proof at room temperature for 1–1½ hours, or until the dough has risen about 2.5 cm (1 in) above the top of the tin.

10. Preheat the oven to 200°C (400°F). For the best rise, place a baking tray half-filled with hot water in the bottom of the oven as it preheats. This will create a steamy environment so the bread can rise to its full potential, but it's not compulsory.

11. Brush the top of the loaf with a little milk or water, then bake for 30–35 minutes, or until the top of the bread is a deep golden brown. If you added a steam tray to the oven, remove it after 15 minutes and finish baking without it.

12. Once baked, remove the bread from the oven. Leave it to cool in the tin for 5 minutes, then run a knife around the edges of the tin and flip the bread out onto a cooling rack. The bread should sound hollow when tapped on the bottom. Let it cool completely before slicing and enjoying. See page 80 for instructions on storing, freezing and reheating sandwich bread.

Optional: When the bread is still piping hot, you can run a little pat of butter over the top of the crust. This will help to keep the crust of the bread nice and soft, and will give it an attractive sheen.

Make it Ahead – Overnight Sandwich Bread

Making these four adjustments to the recipe will allow you to make the dough a day before you plan to bake it.

- Use less yeast: Reduce the yeast quantity to 8 g (2 teaspoons). The yeast is reduced because the dough will be fermenting for a longer period.
- Reduce proofing time in the bowl to 45 minutes.
- Refrigerate overnight: After the loaf has been shaped and placed into the tin, cover it with cling film (plastic wrap) and leave it in the refrigerator overnight.
- Allow more time for proofing before baking: The next day, remove the tin from the fridge and proof at room temperature for about 2 hours before baking as normal. The dough needs a little extra time to rise at this stage, since it will be starting from cold.

Wholewheat Sandwich Bread

Technically speaking, this dough is *slightly* different to the Sandwich Bread dough that this chapter is built upon, but I've bent the rules for good reason. One of the most common questions I get about my recipes is: 'Can I make this using wholewheat flour?' The answer is usually 'YES!', but a few tiny adjustments to the dough itself are required. The result is a heartier and slightly nuttier-flavoured loaf that is particularly good toasted and spread with salted butter and honey.

**MAKES 1 LOAF,
12 SLICES**

(V)

300 g (10½ oz/scant 2½ cups) wholewheat flour
200 g (7 oz/generous 1½ cups) white bread flour
80 ml (2¾ fl oz/generous 5 tablespoons) milk
30 g (2 tablespoons) salted butter, plus extra for greasing
250 ml (8½ fl oz/1 cup) warm water
12 g (1 tablespoon) instant yeast
15 g (1 tablespoon) honey, sugar or agave syrup
8 g (1¾ teaspoons) fine sea salt
neutral-tasting oil such as vegetable oil, or softened butter, for oiling the bowl

1. Follow the Sandwich Bread method on page 82, using the slightly amended ingredients list here.

Tips for Wholewheat Bread Dough:

- Wholewheat bread dough typically rises a bit quicker, so it may only need about 45 minutes in the bowl before shaping and it may need a little less time rising in the tin too.
- Be sure to liberally butter the baking tin as the wholewheat loaf can sometimes stick a bit more than the white version.
- If the wholewheat dough feels a bit sticky after it's been shaped, you can dust a bit of wholewheat flour over the top of it to avoid the cloth or cling film (plastic wrap) from sticking to it during its final proof.
- Sometimes wholewheat bread can brown a bit quicker while baking. If you notice this happening, tent some aluminium foil over the top of the bread for the final 5–10 minutes of bake time.

TIP:

If you'd like a honey wholewheat loaf, increase the honey quantity to 3 tablespoons and reduce the water quantity to 235 ml (8 fl oz/scant 1 cup).

Grilled Nectarine, Burrata & Hot Honey Toast

This toast is what summer lunchtime dreams are made of. The grilled fruit and pickled onions provide a punch of acidity to balance out the richness of the burrata. If you've never tried fruit as a topping for toast, now is the time.

MAKES 1 GENEROUSLY TOPPED TOAST

1 nectarine or peach, cut into wedges
extra virgin olive oil, for drizzling
1 large slice of Sandwich Bread (page 82)
75 g (2½ oz) burrata or Homemade Stracciatella (page 70)
1½ tablespoons Pink Pickled Onions (see right)
fresh basil leaves, to garnish
Homemade Hot Honey, for drizzling (page 152)
flaky sea salt, to taste

1. Lightly coat the nectarine or peach wedges with extra virgin olive oil. Heat a large frying pan or griddle pan over a medium–high heat, then cook the fruit for 2–3 minutes on each side until caramelised.
2. Meanwhile, drizzle the slice of bread with a little extra virgin olive oil on each side, then place it into the hot pan, away from the nectarine wedges. Cook to your desired level of crispiness on both sides.
3. Spread the burrata onto the warm toast, and sprinkle a little flaky sea salt onto the cheese. Pile on the grilled fruit, then top with some pickled onions and fresh basil leaves. Drizzle with hot honey to finish and serve.

Pink Pickled Onions

MAKES 1 LARGE JAR

170 ml (5¾ fl oz/scant ¾ cup) white wine vinegar
30 g (1 tablespoon) granulated sugar
8 g (½ tablespoon) fine sea salt
30 ml (2 tablespoons) water
2 medium red onions, thinly sliced
12 whole black peppercorns (optional)

1. In a small saucepan, stir together the vinegar, sugar, salt and water. Bring to a gentle boil, then reduce the heat to low and simmer and stir until the sugar and salt have dissolved completely.
2. Pack the thinly sliced onions and peppercorns (if using) into a large sterilised glass jar. Pour the hot vinegar mixture over the onions and top up with additional hot water if the onions aren't completely submerged in the pickling liquid.
3. Leave to cool completely before sealing with the lid. These will keep in the refrigerator, sealed, for up to 2 weeks. The onions are ready to use after 20 minutes, but they are even better after a couple of hours, once they've had a chance to properly pickle.

TOPPING TIP:

I always have a jar of these pink onions in my fridge. Be sure to try them on my Ultimate Avocado Toast (page 93) or on the Roasted Pumpkin Pizza (page 154).

You could also try using a slice of the Easy Dutch Oven Bread (page 58) as the base for this toast.

The Ultimate Avocado Toast

I'll be the first to admit that I think avocado toast is a bit overplayed. But this?!
This avocado toast has won me over – and I think you'll love it too.

**MAKES 1 LOADED
SLICE OF TOAST**

1 thick slice of Sandwich
  Bread (page 82)
½–1 avocado, depending on
  size
liberal sprinkle of Everything
  Bagel Seasoning (see
  below)
2 tablespoons Pink Pickled
  Onions (page 90)
1 tablespoon feta cheese,
  crumbled (optional)
extra virgin olive oil, for
  drizzling
flaky sea salt and freshly
  ground black pepper

1. Toast or grill the bread to your liking.
2. While the bread is toasting, scoop the avocado half/halves from the skin(s) using a spoon. Slice into thin strips and then press the knife down slightly on the slices to create a pretty fanned-out effect.
3. Arrange the avocado slices on the toast, and top with a good sprinkling of the Everything Bagel Seasoning, along with a little flaky sea salt and black pepper. Add plenty of Pink Pickled Onions, followed by the crumbled feta, and finish with another sprinkling of Everything Bagel Seasoning and a good drizzle of extra virgin olive oil. Enjoy.

Everything Bagel Seasoning

**MAKES ABOUT
100 G (3½ OZ/
¾ CUP)**

3 tablespoons white
  sesame seeds
2 tablespoons black
  sesame seeds
2 tablespoons dried
  minced garlic (also
  called dried chopped
  garlic)
2 tablespoons dried
  minced onion
2 teaspoons poppy seeds
4 teaspoons flaky sea salt

The texture of the dried minced garlic and onion really does matter here – be sure to use the chunkier minced versions of these rather than powdered granules.

1. In a small bowl, mix all the ingredients together.
2. Store in a lidded jar or container in a cool, dry cupboard for up to 6 months.

TOPPING TIP:

Be sure to try the Everything
Bagel Seasoning as a topping
for the Brilliant Bagels on
page 118. This seasoning
is also great dimpled into
focaccia before baking.

Borough Market Cheese Toastie

When we were first married, my husband and I lived in Bermondsey, London. Our flat was a short stroll from lots of microbreweries and food markets, including the best-known food market in London: Borough Market. One of the most iconic spots at Borough Market is Kappacasein, a stall famous for their raclette and toasties. This is my attempt at recreating their cheese toastie – but if you ever find yourself in London, you must try the real deal!

**MAKES 1 VERY
CHEESY TOASTIE**

(V)

45 g (1½ oz/scant ½ cup)
  mature Cheddar, grated
45 g (1½ oz/scant ½ cup)
  grated mozzarella
2 tablespoons of your choice
  of finely diced leek, red
  onion, white onion, spring
  onion (scallion), chives*
2 slices Sandwich Bread
  (page 82)
salted butter, softened,
  for spreading

* I watched an interview of
the owner of Kappacasein
making one of their famous
toasties, and he said they
include the entire onion
family. I'd recommend
adding a good pinch of at
least three of the types of
onion listed above.

1. In a bowl, mix the grated cheeses with your chosen onions and set aside.
2. Heat a medium–large frying pan over a medium–low heat.
3. Butter the bread slices, then turn over and top one of the unbuttered sides with the cheese-and-onion mixture, making sure it reaches all the way to the edges. Top with the other bread slice, buttered side on the outside, and squish the sandwich together tightly before transferring it to the preheated frying pan. Don't worry if a bit of the cheese spills over the sides: the crispy cheese bits that cook onto the crust are most desirable!
4. Once it's in the pan, place a piece of baking parchment over the buttery top side of the sandwich, then place something heavy on top of it to act as a panini press.
5. Press down to flatten the sandwich a little, then cook for 3–4 minutes, or until the underside is perfectly toasty and golden. Flip the sandwich over, then replace the parchment and makeshift weight. Press down again and cook for another 3–4 minutes, or until the bread is golden and the cheese is completely melted.
6. Cut diagonally and devour immediately.

California-style BLT with Homemade Ranch Dressing

As an avocado-loving California girl, this is my ultimate version of a BLT. The creamy avocado and homemade ranch dressing elevate this BLT (or BLART, if we're being technical!) to the next level. Ranch dressing isn't a big thing in the UK, so when that craving from home hits, this is the recipe I use to get my fix from afar.

MAKES 1 SANDWICH

6 rashers streaky smoked bacon
2 thick slices Sandwich Bread (page 82)
4 tablespoons Homemade Ranch Dressing (see below), for spreading
handful of shredded iceberg lettuce
2–3 ripe tomato slices
½ medium avocado, thinly sliced
flaky sea salt and freshly ground black pepper

1. Cook the bacon in a frying pan over a medium–high heat until crisp, turning it when needed and removing from the pan once it's reached your desired level of crispiness. When it's almost ready, toast the bread.
2. Slather both slices of toast with the ranch dressing, then pile the lettuce onto the bottom slice of bread and drizzle a little more dressing over the lettuce. Arrange the tomatoes on top of the lettuce and season, then top with the avocado, followed by the bacon. Season again, then top with the other piece of toast. Slice in half and enjoy immediately.

Homemade Ranch Dressing

MAKES 360 G (12½ OZ/1½ CUPS)

150 g (5 oz/⅔ cup) mayonnaise
130 g (4½ oz/½ cup) thick, full-fat Greek yoghurt or sour cream
2 small garlic cloves, roughly chopped
1½ teaspoons onion granules
2 spring onions (scallions), roughly chopped
1 tablespoon milk
1 teaspoon red wine vinegar
1 teaspoon fresh lemon juice
¼ teaspoon granulated sugar
½ teaspoon flaky sea salt
30 twists of freshly ground black pepper
2 dashes of your favourite hot sauce (I like Tabasco)
1 tablespoon roughly chopped flat-leaf parsley

1. Combine all the ingredients except the parsley in a blender and blend until smooth. Add the parsley and then pulse again briefly, but make sure that some flecks of green remain. Taste and adjust the seasoning to your liking.
2. This dressing can be stored in an airtight container in the refrigerator for up to a week. It may thicken up in the fridge, but you can thin it out with a splash of milk if needed.

TOPPING TIP:

Add a grilled chicken breast to make this a California-style club sandwich.

TIP:

This dressing makes a great dip for the Garlic Butter Breadsticks on page 180.

Pesto Chicken Melt

My parents owned diner-style restaurants when I was growing up. From the age of 10, I earned pocket money by sweeping floors and clearing tables on the weekends and by the time I was a teenager, I was promoted to waitress. Eventually, I took on management shifts while I was studying at university. From the start, this Pesto Chicken Melt was one of the most popular sandwiches on their menu, and I swear it's because of the Parmesan-crusted bread. Once you try grilling your bread like this, you'll never go back.

MAKES 1 SANDWICH

1 chicken breast (approx. 185 g /6½ oz)
extra virgin olive oil, for drizzling
½ red (bell) pepper, cut into thick strips
2 slices Sandwich Bread (page 82)
1 tablespoon salted butter, melted
2 tablespoons Parmesan, finely grated
3 tablespoons Fresh Basil Pesto (page 155) or store-bought pesto
2 slices provolone or mozzarella
flaky sea salt and freshly ground black pepper

FOR THE ROCKET SALAD
handful of rocket (arugula)
drizzle of extra virgin olive oil
tiny squeeze of lemon juice
a few Parmesan shavings

1. Preheat the oven to 200°C (400°F). Place the chicken breast on a small baking tray and drizzle with extra virgin olive oil, then season with salt and pepper. Bake for around 20 minutes, or until the juices of the chicken run clear and the internal temperature has reached 74°C (165°F).
2. Meanwhile, lightly coat the red pepper slices with extra virgin olive oil and season with salt and pepper. Add them to the tray with the chicken for the final 12 minutes of roasting time.
3. When the chicken and peppers are nearly finished baking, preheat a large frying pan over a medium heat and coat with a drizzle of extra virgin olive oil.
4. Brush each slice of the sandwich bread with the melted butter and press the grated Parmesan into the butter (this will be the outside of the sandwich). Spread the other side of each slice with pesto, using about 1 tablespoon on each slice.
5. Lay the bread into the preheated pan, Parmesan-side down, and place the sliced cheese on top of one of the slices. Leave to cook for 4–5 minutes until golden and crispy.
6. While the bread is grilling in the pan, toss together the salad ingredients in a small bowl and season with a pinch each of salt and pepper.
7. Once the Parmesan-crusted bread is golden and crispy, remove it from the pan. Place the warm chicken breast on top of the provolone or mozzarella and top with the remaining pesto, followed by the salad and roasted pepper slices. Top with the other slice of Parmesan-crusted bread and squish the two sides of the sandwich together. Halve diagonally and enjoy!

TIP:

The next time you make a grilled cheese sandwich, use the method above to give the bread a Parmesan crust.

Good ol' Buttered Toast – But Make it Homemade

In my opinion, there is nothing – and I mean nothing – better than fresh homemade bread with good salted butter. So, with that in mind, I'm about to suggest you try making your own butter. If you have a stand mixer or a handheld mixer, it will take you less than 10 minutes to make homemade butter. I know it sounds crazy, but just give it a try!

MAKES 160 G (5½ OZ) DELICIOUS HOMEMADE BUTTER

300 ml (10 fl oz/1¼ cups) double (heavy) cream*
flaky sea salt, to taste – I use about ¾ teaspoon

TO SERVE

thick slices of Sandwich Bread (page 82), toasted

* Buy the best-quality cream you can find. Cream from grass-fed cows will result in a more flavourful, creamy and yellow butter because of the quality high-fat dairy these cows are able to produce.

FLAVOURED BUTTER IDEAS:

If you'd like to try making a flavoured butter, here are some ideas to get you started:
- smoked sea salt
- garlic & herbs
- cinnamon & sugar
- honey & sea salt
- cinnamon, honey & sea salt
- Parmesan & black pepper
- sun-dried tomato, basil & Parmesan
- miso & honey
- chimichurri (parsley, coriander/cilantro, oregano, chilli, garlic & sea salt)

1. Remove the cream from the refrigerator about 30 minutes before you intend to make the butter.
2. Pour the cream into a large mixing bowl or the bowl of a stand mixer. If you're using a stand mixer, attach the whisk attachment. If you're using a handheld mixer, use the beater attachment.
3. Whip the cream at a medium–high speed. Keep whipping it past the whipped cream stage, and only stop when the solid butterfat has completely separated from the buttermilk. It will be obvious when this happens, because you'll notice the bowl will contain a solid blob resembling butter (butterfat), sitting in some white, cloudy liquid (buttermilk).
4. Fill a medium-sized bowl with water and ice.
5. Using clean hands, grab the solid butter from the bowl and squeeze it tightly, allowing any excess liquid to fall into the bowl of buttermilk below. Repeat this process until you're no longer able to squeeze any liquid from the solid butter.
6. Submerge the solid butter in the iced water and squeeze it a few more times to wash away any buttermilk. If the ice water is clear after this step, then the butter is no longer retaining buttermilk. If the water is cloudy, drain it off, refill with fresh cold water and repeat this process until the water remains clear.
7. Transfer the butter onto a piece of non-stick baking parchment and spread it out over the paper. Sprinkle the flaky sea salt over the butter and then mash it all up with a spoon so that the seasoning is evenly distributed. If you plan to make a flavoured butter (see ideas left), it's best to place the butter into a bowl and stir in any additions before moving on to the next step.
8. Shape the butter into a cylindrical log and then wrap the parchment tightly around it, twisting both ends of the log to seal. The butter can be used immediately, or it can be stored in the fridge for up to 2 weeks.
9. To serve, slather some thick slices of toasted Sandwich Bread with your beautiful homemade butter and enjoy.

Spicy, Jammy Eggs on Toast with Spring Onion Cream Cheese

These eggs on toast pack a serious flavour punch and can be made within 10 minutes for a quick go-to breakfast, lunch or dinner.

SERVES 1–2, DEPENDING ON APPETITE!

2 large eggs
2 thick slices Sandwich Bread (page 82)
crispy chilli oil, for drizzling
finely diced chives, to garnish

FOR THE SPRING ONION CREAM CHEESE
5 tablespoons cream cheese
1 tablespoon finely diced spring onions (scallions)
1½ teaspoons finely diced chives
⅛ teaspoon garlic granules
pinch of flaky sea salt

1. Bring a small pot of water to a rolling boil and gently lower the eggs into the water with a large spoon. Set a timer for 7½ minutes and maintain the water at a rolling boil. Note that the size of your eggs will impact how long it takes to cook a 'jammy' egg. The sweet spot is typically 7–8 minutes, so if you like them on the runnier side, reduce the timer by 30 seconds.
2. Meanwhile, in a small bowl, stir together the ingredients for the spring onion cream cheese.
3. While the eggs are boiling, fill a medium-sized bowl with cold water and add some ice cubes. When the timer goes off, remove the eggs from the boiling water and plunge them into the ice bath to stop them cooking.
4. Toast the bread slices until they're a deep golden brown. Spread each slice with half of the spring onion cream cheese. Peel the eggs and cut them into quarters, then smash them slightly onto the toast. Sprinkle with flaky sea salt, drizzle with crispy chilli oil (as much as you can handle!), and scatter over some chives to finish before serving.

TOPPING TIP:

Pair the spring onion cream cheese with my Brilliant Bagels (page 118).

Cinnamon Sugar Toast

This toast transports me back to sleepovers at my best friend's house when I was in elementary school. Her mom used to serve us cinnamon sugar toast while we sat in front of the TV watching Saturday morning cartoons. If your childhood didn't include this, I urge you to make up for lost time. Slices of bread are slathered with cinnamon sugar butter and baked in the oven until the exterior is brûléed and the interior is squidgy from the melted butter. Be warned: you will not be able to stop at one slice!

MAKES 4 SLICES

Ⓥ

60 g (2 oz/4 tablespoons) salted butter, softened
4 tablespoons granulated or caster (superfine) sugar
1½ teaspoons ground cinnamon
¼ teaspoon vanilla extract
tiny pinch of flaky sea salt
4 slices Sandwich Bread (page 82)

1. Preheat the oven to 180°C (350°F).
2. Combine the softened butter, sugar, cinnamon, vanilla and salt in a small bowl and mix until super smooth.
3. Spread a quarter of the butter mixture onto each slice of bread, ensuring it reaches the very edges of the bread.
4. Place on a baking tray, butter-side up, and bake for 10 minutes.
5. Adjust the oven setting to grill/broil or transfer to the grill, and cook for an additional 2–3 minutes. Watch closely so it doesn't burn. The toast is ready when the sugar-and-butter mixture has started to caramelise. Enjoy warm from the oven.

TOPPING TIP:

Once the toast is out of the oven, add a layer of cream cheese, some thinly sliced apples, and some fresh berries or jam to make it 'cheesecake toast'.

Salt & Pepper Croutons

This is arguably the easiest way to give new life to a hunk of staling bread. My kids love salad, and ask for it for dinner all the time – with one major caveat. 'It has to have those yummy croutons on top!' Let's be honest, making a quick batch of these croutons is a small price to pay if it means my kids are happy to eat a big bowl of raw veggies for dinner.

MAKES 150 G (5 OZ/ 2 CUPS)

200 g (7 oz) Sandwich Bread (page 82), cubed to desired size
2 tablespoons extra virgin olive oil or melted butter
¼ teaspoon flaky sea salt
20 twists of freshly ground pepper

1. Preheat the oven to 200°C (400°F).
2. Tip the bread cubes into a large mixing bowl.
3. In a small bowl, whisk together the olive oil, flaky sea salt and freshly ground pepper, then drizzle this mixture over the cubed bread. Toss together using your hands to ensure that each piece of bread has been coated in the mixture.
4. Spread out the bread pieces in a single layer on a large baking sheet and bake for 18–22 minutes, or until the croutons are golden brown and crispy throughout.
5. These will keep in a sealed container or zip-top storage bag at room temperature for up to 2 weeks.

THINK OUTSIDE THE (BREAD)BOX:

Turn these croutons into tasty breadcrumbs by blitzing them in a blender or food processor.

Thanksgiving Stuffing
with Homemade Croutons

It probably won't come as a surprise that my favourite class in high school was Culinary Arts. The teacher, Mrs Ganister (affectionately nicknamed 'Gani' by her students) was like a second mom to me, and she is still in my life to this day. One November, she taught our class how to make this stuffing, and I have made it every Thanksgiving since – a whopping 20 years! If you don't celebrate Thanksgiving, this stuffing would make an excellent side to accompany a special roast dinner. Served alongside roast turkey, it has become a Christmas Day favourite for our UK family.

SERVES 16

150 g (5 oz/10 tablespoons) salted butter, plus extra for greasing
2 tablespoons extra virgin olive oil
3 tablespoons chicken seasoning*
1 loaf (about 800 g/1 lb 12 oz) of Sandwich Bread (page 82), cut or torn into crouton-sized cubes
2 large onions, finely diced
6 celery stalks, finely diced
1.4 litres (47 fl oz/scant 6 cups) chicken or vegetable stock (broth)
2 large eggs
6 thyme sprigs, leaves picked
3–4 fresh sage leaves, julienned
sea salt and freshly ground black pepper, to taste

* Try to find a chicken seasoning that contains most of the following ingredients: garlic, onion, salt, black pepper, red or green (bell) pepper, parsley, paprika and some sort of citrus peel. My teacher used McCormick's Montreal Chicken Seasoning, and I agree, it is the best! I also like Bart's Chicken Seasoning.

1. Preheat the oven to 190°C (375°F).
2. Line two large baking trays with foil, and dollop 2 tablespoons of the butter onto each tray, along with 1 tablespoon of olive oil. Sprinkle 1 tablespoon of chicken seasoning over the top of the butter and oil on each tray, and add some freshly ground black pepper. Place the trays in the oven for 4–5 minutes until the butter has melted completely.
3. Remove the trays from the oven and stir the butter, oil and seasoning together. Divide the cubes of bread between the trays and toss to coat them in the butter mixture. Return the trays to the oven and bake for 25–30 minutes, or until the croutons are completely crunchy and golden. Depending on how evenly your oven cooks, you may want to swap the trays over after about 20 minutes.
4. When the croutons have nearly finished baking, you can get started on the onions and celery. Melt 4 tablespoons of the butter in an extra-large frying pan or a large wok over a medium heat (you need a pan big enough to hold all the croutons). Add the onions and celery, along with the remaining 1 tablespoon of chicken seasoning and some freshly ground black pepper. Cook for about 12 minutes until the celery has softened and the onions are translucent.
5. In a large bowl or jug, whisk together the stock and eggs. If you're making the stock from cubes, ensure it isn't too hot, as this can scramble the eggs.
6. Reduce the heat below the frying pan to low and add 1 litre (34 fl oz/ 4 cups) of the stock mixture to the onions and celery. Add the croutons and herbs to the pan and stir until all the liquid has been absorbed. Let the croutons sit for a few minutes more to soften up.
7. Use a wooden spoon or potato masher to break up the croutons into smaller pieces. This will take a little while, but you'll see how these smaller pieces will help to bind the stuffing together nicely. Gradually add the remaining stock, allowing the bread to fully absorb the new stock each time before adding more – you may not need all of it, or you may need a touch more. Keep breaking up the croutons until the stuffing has reached your desired texture. Taste and season with salt and pepper, or more chicken seasoning if you feel it needs it.

8. Grease two baking dishes with butter. I use two 20 cm (8 in) square dishes, but the size doesn't really matter as long as there is plenty of surface area on top so the stuffing can crisp up.

9. Dot 1 tablespoon of butter over the top of each dish of stuffing and bake, uncovered, for 25–30 minutes, or until the stuffing is hot throughout and the top layer is golden and crispy. Serve.

Customise your stuffing

This stuffing makes an excellent base to build upon. Feel free to add cooked sausage, dried fruits or nuts, or swap in different herbs to suit your tastes. Add these right after you've added the croutons to the stock.

Make ahead

The croutons can be baked and stored in an airtight storage container or sealed storage bag for up to a week before you plan to assemble the stuffing. The prepared stuffing can be wrapped up in its dish and refrigerated for up to 2 days before you plan to bake it. Remember to dot the butter on top before baking. You may need to add a few extra minutes of bake time if you're cooking it straight from the refrigerator.

THINK OUTSIDE THE (BREAD)BOX:

You can also use a slab of Same-day Focaccia (page 22) or a loaf of Easy Dutch Oven Bread (page 58) to make the croutons for this recipe.

English Muffins

English muffins, muffins, breakfast muffins, oven-bottom muffins... there are so many names for this type of bread. No matter what you call them, these griddled muffins act as the perfect base for eggs Benedict or your favourite breakfast sandwich.

MAKES 10 MUFFINS

1 batch Sandwich Bread
   dough (page 82)
3 tablespoons fine semolina
   or fine cornmeal, for
   coating

1. Prepare the Sandwich Bread dough up to the end of step 6 on page 85. Once it has finished proofing in the bowl, tip the dough onto your work surface and cut it into 10 equal-sized pieces – they should weigh about 85 g (3 oz) each.
2. Shape each piece into a tight dough ball. The easiest way of doing this is to gather all the sides of the dough into the middle to form a ball shape, then flip it so the side with the seams is underneath. Now cup your hand over the dough ball and move your hand around in a circular motion while putting a slight pressure on the dough ball underneath. The dough should tighten up into a smooth-looking ball. Repeat this with the remaining dough.
3. Tip the fine semolina onto a small plate. Flatten each dough ball into a disc about 9 cm (3½ in) in diameter and then dip both flattened sides into the semolina. Place on a tray and cover with an inverted tray of the same size or some loosely draped cling film (plastic wrap). Leave to proof at room temperature for 30–45 minutes, or until they've puffed up nicely.
4. Heat a large non-stick or cast-iron frying pan over a medium–low heat. Place five of the dough discs into the pan, then cover with a lid. Cook for 5–7 minutes on one side, then remove the lid, flip them over, replace the lid and continue cooking for another 3–5 minutes on the other side. The muffins should be crispy, griddled and golden brown on both sides. Remove to a cooling rack and repeat with the remaining muffins.
5. Leave to cool for at least 10 minutes, then split the muffins in half, pierce the entire perimeter of the muffin with a fork and then gently pry open.
6. These are best when toasted. They can be stored in an airtight container for up to 3 days, and can also be frozen; just be sure to split before freezing so you can easily toast them from frozen.

Giant Soft Pretzels

Soft with a slightly crisp bite, these doughy, buttery and salty pretzels taste just like the ones found in shopping malls and amusement parks. My dad is the number one bread-lover in my life – whenever he is sent to the store to get a baguette, you can bet that he will tear into one end of it before he gets home, turning it around in the bag to hide the evidence. He has an incredible fondness for soft pretzels, too, so Dad, this recipe is for you...

MAKES 6 GIANT PRETZELS

1 batch Sandwich Bread
dough (page 82)
75 g (2½ oz/⅓ cup) salted
butter, melted, plus extra
for greasing
coarse salt or flaky sea salt

FOR THE DIP SOLUTION
900 ml (30 fl oz/scant
4 cups) hot water
6 tablespoons bicarbonate
of soda (baking soda)

1. Prepare the Sandwich Bread dough up to the end of step 6, page 85. Once it has finished proofing in the bowl, preheat the oven to 220°C (425°F) and grease two large baking trays measuring 33 × 46 cm (13 × 18 in) with salted butter.
2. Make the dip solution by combining the hot water and bicarbonate of soda in a large mixing bowl. Stir until the bicarb has dissolved, then set aside.
3. Tip the dough onto your work surface and divide it into 6 pieces, each weighing roughly 140 g (5 oz).
4. Take one piece of dough and roll it into a long rope measuring about 80 cm (32 in) long. The best way to do this is to grab the portion of dough with both hands and stretch both ends to lengthen it, before rolling it into a rope with an even thickness throughout.
5. To shape it into a pretzel, arrange the rope in a large 'U' shape on the work surface. Grab the ends of the dough and cross them over each other to make an 'X'. Cross the ends over each other once more. You should have formed a twisted section near the ends of the dough, but the bottom of the 'U' should have remained the same shape. Fold the ends of the dough down to the bottom of the 'U' shape and gently press to join. Repeat this process with the remaining portions of dough.
6. Give the dip solution a quick stir and grab a cooling rack. Pick up your first pretzel by grabbing the part where the ends of the rope have joined to the bottom of the 'U'. Dip it into the solution, then place on the cooling rack to allow the excess solution to drip away. Repeat with the remaining pretzels, then place them on the prepared baking trays and sprinkle with salt.
7. Bake for 10–14 minutes, swapping the trays halfway through so they bake evenly. While they're baking, melt the butter in a small saucepan over a low heat.
8. Once the pretzels are golden brown, remove them from the oven and brush them with melted butter while they're still on the baking trays. Wiggle them around on the tray so the bottoms can soak up any excess butter that has dripped down the sides.
9. These pretzels are at their best when they are fresh from the oven. Store any leftover pretzels in an airtight container or plastic storage bag for up to two days at room temperature, then warm up in the microwave for about 30 seconds before eating.

Soft Pretzel Bites

I'll admit that it can be a little tricky to get the hang of shaping the Giant Soft Pretzels on page 112, so here is an easier pretzel option that also happens to make a great snack to feed a crowd at parties. If you'd like to make these into pretzel breadsticks, cut each rope into three pieces instead of 12.

MAKES 60 PRETZEL BITES

1 batch Sandwich Bread dough (page 82)
coarse salt or flaky sea salt
75 g (2½ oz) salted butter, plus extra for greasing

FOR THE DIP SOLUTION
900 ml (30 fl oz/scant 4 cups) hot water
6 tablespoons bicarbonate of soda (baking soda)

1. Follow the Giant Soft Pretzels recipe on page 112 up until the end of step 3, inlcuding making the dip solution, then continue with the method below.
2. Roll each of the six pieces of dough into a long rope measuring about 55 cm (18 in) long. Using a pizza cutter, divide each rope into 10 evenly sized pieces. To save time, you can line three ropes up next to one another and roll the pizza cutter through all of them each time. Repeat this process with the remaining three ropes.
3. Give the dip solution a quick stir and grab a cooling rack. Place about 20 dough bites into the dip solution and stir to coat them fully. Remove them with a slotted spoon or sieve, then place them on a cooling rack to allow the excess solution to drip away. Repeat with the remaining pieces of dough, working in batches.
4. Transfer the pretzel bites to the prepared baking trays and spread them out as evenly as possible. Sprinkle them with salt.
5. Bake for 9–12 minutes, swapping the trays halfway through so they bake evenly. While they're baking, melt the butter in a small saucepan over a low heat.
6. Remove the trays from the oven and brush the pretzel bites with the melted butter while they're still on the baking trays. Wiggle the pretzel bites around in the trays so their bottoms can soak up any excess butter that has dripped down the sides.
7. These are at their peak when they are fresh from the oven. Store any leftover pretzel bites in an airtight container or plastic storage bag for up to 2 days at room temperature and warm in the microwave for 15–20 seconds before eating.

TOPPING TIP:

To turn these into cinnamon sugar pretzel bites, omit the sprinkle of salt and toss the bites in cinnamon sugar after they've been coated in butter. To make the cinnamon sugar, mix 100 g (3½ oz/scant ½ cup) granulated sugar with 2 tablespoons ground cinnamon.

Cheesy Garlic Swirls

Move aside cinnamon buns: a savoury version has arrived! Swirled with garlic butter and melted cheese, these fluffy, cloud-like buns are a worthy rival to their sticky, sweet counterpart.

MAKES 12 ROLLS

1 batch Sandwich Bread dough (page 82)
olive oil, for oiling the work surface
200 g (7 oz/2 cups) grated mozzarella
60ml (2 fl oz/¼ cup) double (heavy) cream

FOR THE GARLIC BUTTER
115g (scant 4 oz/½ cup) salted butter, softened, plus extra for greasing
4 garlic cloves, finely minced
30 g (1 oz/½ cup) Parmesan or vegetarian Italian-style hard cheese, finely grated, plus extra to garnish
1 tablespoon finely chopped flat-leaf parsley, plus extra to garnish
freshly ground black pepper

TIP:

These would be excellent served with some Perfect Pizza Sauce (page 161) for dipping!

1. Prepare the Sandwich Bread dough up to the end of step 6 on page 85. As it's proofing in the bowl, prepare the garlic butter by mashing together all the ingredients. If you need to soften the butter, microwave it in 5-second increments until softened. Grease a 23 × 33 cm (9 × 13 in) baking tray with salted butter and set aside.

2. Tip the dough onto a lightly oiled work surface and roll it into a 30 × 40 cm (12 × 16 in) rectangle. Spread the garlic butter evenly across the dough, leaving a 1 cm (½ in) gap along the top of the long side of the rectangle. Sprinkle the mozzarella over the garlic butter in an even layer and press it in to stick.

3. Roll up the dough lengthways into a tight cylinder, and pinch together the seams to seal. Rotate the cylindrical log on the work surface so the seam is at the bottom. Using a butter knife, make little indentations to mark out where you will cut it into 12 equal pieces.

4. The neatest way of cutting the dough is to use unflavoured dental floss. Simply slide a long piece of floss under the roll of dough and align it with one of your cutting indentations, then cross the ends of the floss over each other and pull in opposite directions until you've made a clean cut through the roll. You can also use a knife or dough scraper to cut, but the rolls can get a bit squished.

5. Arrange the rolls swirl-side up on the prepared baking tray, evenly spaced apart from one another – 4 along the long side of the tray and 3 along the shorter. Cover with an inverted tray of the same size, or some loosely draped cling film (plastic wrap) and leave to proof at room temperature for 45 minutes to 1 hour.

6. Preheat the oven to 180°C (350°F). While it is preheating, place a large baking tray on the middle rack – make sure it's larger than the tray you're baking your rolls in.

7. When the rolls have finished proofing, brush the cream over their tops and sides, then place the baking tray on top of the large, preheated tray in the oven (this extra tray will catch any garlic butter that may spill over the sides while baking).

8. Bake for 32–38 minutes until the rolls are crisping up and the cheese swirl on top of each roll has turned golden brown. Once out of the oven, sprinkle some grated Parmesan and chopped parsley over the top before serving warm. The rolls can be kept in a lidded container or sealed zip-top bag in the fridge for up to 3 days. To reheat, microwave for 30 seconds. These also freeze really well – cool completely, separate the rolls and transfer to a large freezer bag. To reheat, microwave for about 1 minute, or until hot in the middle.

Brilliant Bagels

This bagel recipe is dedicated to my beautiful mom. About a decade ago, I made homemade bagels for my parents during one of their many visits to London, and my mom still talks about how those bagels were among the best things she's ever eaten. This version calls for Sandwich Bread dough instead of an authentic bagel dough, but they certainly hit the spot when a bagel craving strikes.

MAKES 8 BAGELS

1 batch Sandwich Bread
  dough (page 82)
plain (all-purpose) flour, for
  dusting
extra virgin olive oil or
  vegetable oil, for greasing
3 litres (104 fl oz/12 cups)
  water
2 tablespoons bicarbonate
  of soda (baking soda)
1 tablespoon light brown
  sugar
1 egg white
toppings or flavourings of
  your choice (see below)

1. Prepare the Sandwich Bread dough up to the end of step 6 on page 85. Once it has finished proofing in the bowl, tip the dough onto your work surface and cut it into 8 equal-sized pieces – they should weigh around 105 g (3¾ oz) each.

2. Dust the work surface with a little flour and shape each piece into a tight dough ball. The easiest way of doing this is to gather all the sides of the dough into the middle to form a ball shape, then flip it so the side with the seams is underneath. Now cup your hand over the dough ball and move your hand around in a circular motion while putting a slight pressure on the dough ball underneath. The dough should tighten up into a smooth-looking ball. Repeat this with all the other dough balls.

3. Flour your hands and poke a hole through the centre of one of the dough balls with your finger. Twirl the bagel around both index fingers until the hole in the middle has stretched out to about 4 cm (1½ in) wide. Repeat with the other dough balls and place the bagels on a lightly floured tray. Cover with a piece of cling film (plastic wrap) or a very lightly dampened tea towel and leave to proof for 45 minutes–1 hour.

4. About 10 minutes before the end of the proofing time, preheat the oven to 220°C (430°F) and line one large (33 × 46 cm/13 × 18 in) or two medium (23 × 33 cm/9 × 13 in) baking trays with baking parchment. Brush the parchment lightly with olive oil or vegetable oil.

5. In a large pot, bring the water to a gentle boil. Add the bicarbonate of soda and brown sugar, and stir together until dissolved, keeping the water at a gentle boil.

6. Now it's time to boil the bagels. Grab a cooling rack so you have somewhere to put them when they come out of the water. Carefully place four of the bagels into the water and boil the first side for 30–40 seconds, then flip and boil for an additional 30–40 seconds on the other side. Use a large slotted spatula or skimmer to remove the bagels from the water and transfer to the cooling rack. Repeat with the remaining bagels.

7. Once all the bagels have been boiled, arrange them on the prepared baking tray(s). I like to scatter a sprinkling of seeds, bagel seasoning or a little grated cheese onto the spaces on the tray where each bagel will be placed so that seasonings or toppings will bake into both sides of the bagel.

8. Lightly brush some lightly beaten egg white over the top and sides of each bagel. Liberally sprinkle on any seasonings or seeds you wish to add, then give them a pat to make sure they're stuck on.

9. Bake for 15–20 minutes, or until the bagels are golden brown all over. Bagels with cheese on top may need an extra couple of minutes. If you are baking them on more than one tray, swap the trays around in the oven after about 10 minutes to ensure even baking.

10. Enjoy the bagels warm from the oven with your favourite fillings. Use within 3 days – they're best toasted if not fresh. To store, place in a plastic zip-top bag or lidded container at room temperature, or in the fridge if topped with cheese. If you'd like to freeze them, slice down the middle and place in a large freezer bag.

**TOPPING
SUGGESTIONS:**

• Everything Bagel
  Seasoning (page 93)
• Cheddar cheese
• jalapeños & Cheddar
  cheese
• mixed seeds
• poppy seeds
• sesame seeds
• flaky sea salt

Burger Buns

The next time you're hosting a barbecue, why not make your own burger buns?
You can use this recipe to make hot dog buns, too: just see the note below the recipe
for a slightly different dough-shaping technique.

**MAKES 9 BURGER
BUNS**

(V)

1 batch Sandwich Bread
    dough (page 82)
extra virgin olive oil or canola
    oil, for oiling the work
    surface
1 egg
1 tablespoon water
2 tablespoons sesame seeds
    (optional)

1. Prepare the Sandwich Bread dough up to the end of step 6 on page 85 and line a 33 × 46 cm (13 × 18 in) baking tray with baking parchment.
2. Once the dough has finished proofing in the bowl, tip it onto a lightly oiled work surface and cut it into 9 equal-sized pieces – they should weigh about 95 g (scant 3½ oz) each. Adjust the size depending on the size of burgers you'll be cooking; you can make them smaller for sliders if needed.
3. Shape each piece into a tight dough ball. The easiest way of doing this is to gather all the sides of the dough into the middle to form a ball shape, then flip it so the side with the seams is underneath. Now cup your hand over the dough ball and move your hand around in a circular motion while putting a slight pressure on the dough ball underneath. The dough should tighten up into a smooth-looking ball. Repeat this with the remaining dough.
4. Arrange the dough balls on the prepared baking tray. Using your hand, squash each dough ball down until it is shaped more like a thick disc. Cover the tray with a clean tea towel or a piece of cling film (plastic wrap) and leave to proof for about an hour.
5. Preheat the oven to 200°C (400°F).
6. In a small bowl, whisk together the egg and water, then lightly brush this mixture over the tops and sides of each bun. Sprinkle each one with sesame seeds (if using), then bake for 18–20 minutes, or until the tops and bottoms of the buns are golden brown.
7. These buns are best on the day they're baked. You can keep them in plastic storage bags for up to 2 days, but they benefit from being warmed up before using.

For hot dog buns

Once you have divided the dough into 9 equal-sized pieces, roll or press each piece of dough into an oval about 14 cm (5½ in) long. Tightly roll each piece into a cylindrical shape, then pinch both ends of the roll to seal. Place them seam-side down on the prepared baking tray, then proof, egg-wash and bake as stated above.

Honey Butter Dinner Rolls

Dinner rolls don't feature frequently in our home, but around the holidays, a meal feels incomplete without them. The addition of honey butter makes these rolls feel like an extra-special treat, but you can omit the honey for a more classic, buttery dinner-roll experience if you prefer.

MAKES 16 DINNER ROLLS

1 batch Sandwich Bread dough (page 82)
extra virgin olive oil, for oiling the work surface
3 tablespoons salted butter, plus extra for greasing
1½ tablespoons honey

1. Prepare the Sandwich Bread dough up to the end of step 6 on page 85. Once it has finished proofing in the bowl, tip the dough onto a lightly oiled work surface and cut it into 16 equal-sized pieces – they should weigh around 52 g (2 oz) each.
2. Shape each piece into a tight dough ball. The easiest way of doing this is to gather all the sides of the dough into the middle to form a ball shape, then flip it so the side with the seams is underneath. Now cup your hand over the dough ball and move your hand around in a circular motion while putting a slight pressure on the dough ball underneath. The dough should tighten up into a smooth-looking ball. Repeat this with the remaining dough.
3. Liberally butter a 23 × 33 cm (9 × 13 in) baking tray and arrange the rolls in it, in four rows of four. Cover with a clean tea towel or a piece of cling film (plastic wrap) and proof at room temperature for about an hour, or until they've puffed up nicely.
4. When the rolls have almost finished proofing, preheat the oven to 200°C (400°F) and set the rack to the lowest position in the oven.
5. Bake the rolls for 20–28 minutes, or until golden brown on top. Melt the butter and honey together in the microwave or in a small saucepan over a low heat and stir until combined.
6. Brush the honey butter over the tops and sides of the rolls, encouraging it to drip down between the seams where the rolls meet. Allow the butter to soak in for a minute or two before transferring the rolls to a cooling rack so the bottoms don't get soggy. Serve while still warm from the oven. Any leftovers can be wrapped up in a zip-top storage bag and reheated in the microwave for 30 seconds. Alternatively, store any leftovers tightly wrapped in foil and bake (still wrapped in foil) at 180°C (350°F) for 15–18 minutes.

Cinnamon Caramel Monkey Bread

You know the super-soft middle bit of a sticky cinnamon roll? Imagine a ton of those prime bites stuck together. When I tested this recipe, I walked up and down our road presenting unsuspecting neighbours with warm, sticky monkey bread. After politely plucking one dough ball and tasting it, everyone quickly took as many as they could – even our postman couldn't resist!

SERVES 8–10

You'll need a 24 cm (9½ in) Bundt tin or two 900 g (2 lb) loaf tins.

1 batch Sandwich Bread dough (page 82)
115 g (scant 4 oz/½ cup) salted butter, plus extra for greasing
215 g (7½ oz/scant 1¼ cups) soft light brown sugar
1 tablespoon ground cinnamon
120 ml (4 fl oz/½ cup) double (heavy) cream
½ teaspoon vanilla extract

TIP:

If you'd like to enjoy this at brunch, you can assemble it the day beforehand. After all the dough balls have been coated and placed in the tin, cover tightly with cling film and refrigerate overnight. Remove from the refrigerator the next morning and let it rest at room temperature for about 1¼ hours before drizzling with cream and baking as instructed above.

1. Prepare the Sandwich Bread dough up to the end of step 6 on page 85. While it is proofing in the bowl, prepare the Bundt tin (or loaf tins) by greasing it with softened salted butter.
2. Mix together the brown sugar and cinnamon in a medium-sized bowl. Melt the butter in a small bowl in the microwave, or in a small saucepan over a low heat. Set aside to cool.
3. When the dough has finished proofing, tip it out onto a clean work surface and pat it down into a 20 cm (8 in) square. Using a sharp knife or pizza cutter, cut the dough into a grid of 64 pieces, by cutting 8 evenly sized strips in one direction and then 8 strips crossing over in the opposite direction.
4. Roll each piece of dough into a ball using the palms of your hands.
5. Dip one dough ball into the melted butter and let the excess drip away, then roll it in the cinnamon sugar until fully coated. Place the coated dough ball in the prepared Bundt tin and repeat with the remaining dough balls, arranging them close together in the tin in two layers. It takes a little while, but I promise it is worth it! If you don't use all of the butter and sugar, sprinkle the leftovers over the top of the assembled monkey bread before its final proof.
6. Cover with a clean tea towel or a piece of cling film (plastic wrap) and leave to proof for about 1 hour, or until the dough balls have risen almost to the top of the Bundt tin.
7. Preheat the oven to 180°C (350°F) and set the rack in the middle.
8. In a bowl, mix the cream and vanilla extract together, then drizzle it evenly over the top of the monkey bread.
9. Place the Bundt tin on a large baking tray (in case any sugar spills over the sides as it cooks), then bake for 32–36 minutes. The tops of the dough balls should be golden brown and you should notice caramel bubbling around the edges of the tin.
10. Remove from the oven and leave to rest for 5 minutes, before placing a large dinner plate or tray over the rim of the tin and inverting it to release the monkey bread. If you wait too long to do this, the caramel may solidify and make it too sticky to release.
11. Some of the caramel may have accumulated at the top, so use a spoon to spread it evenly over the top and sides of the monkey bread. Allow to cool for a few minutes before devouring warm with those you love! If you find yourself with leftovers, wrap tightly in cling film (plastic wrap) and store in the refrigerator for up to 2 days. Microwave for 15–20 seconds before enjoying.

Chocolatey Rolls

This ultimate weekend treat is sure to please the chocoholics in your life. Imagine gooey cinnamon rolls, but swap out the cinnamon sugar for a rich, chocolatey filling. Bread and chocolate belong together, and these rolls set out to prove it ...

MAKES 12 ROLLS

1 batch Sandwich Bread
  dough (page 82)
2 tablespoons salted butter,
  plus extra for greasing
85 g (3 oz/½ cup) chocolate
  chips
200 g (7 oz/¾ cup) chocolate
  hazelnut spread (I like
  Nutella)
sunflower oil or a neutral-
  tasting oil, for oiling the
  work surface
120 ml (4 fl oz/½ cup) double
  (heavy) cream
1½ tablespoons hot chocolate
  powder

TO FINISH (OPTIONAL)
100 g (3½ oz/⅓ cup)
  chocolate hazelnut spread
2 tablespoons chopped
  hazelnuts

TIP:

To make these in advance,
follow the recipe above up to
step 6, but instead of proofing
at room temperature, cover
the tray tightly with cling film
(plastic wrap) and refrigerate
overnight. In the morning,
remove the tray from the fridge
and proof for 1½ hours at room
temperature before continuing
with the recipe as above.

1. Prepare the Sandwich Bread dough up to the end of step 6 on page 85. Grease a 23 × 33 cm (9 × 13 in) baking tray with salted butter and set aside.
2. When the dough is nearly finished proofing in the bowl, make the chocolate filling. In a medium bowl, microwave the salted butter until it has melted. Stir in the chocolate chips until they melt too, then stir in the chocolate spread.
3. Lightly oil your work surface, then tip the dough onto it. With a rolling pin, roll it into a rectangle measuring roughly 30 × 40 cm (12 × 16 in). Spread the chocolate filling evenly over all the dough, leaving a 1 cm (½ in) gap along the top of the long side of the dough. Roll up the dough lengthways into a tight cylinder; when it is about three-quarters rolled, pull the upper quarter of the dough up to join the roll you've just made. It's easier to do it this way, as there is a lot of chocolate crammed inside and this helps to prevent it from spilling out. Pinch together the seam to seal the roll, then rotate the cylinder so that the seam is on the bottom.
4. Using a butter knife, make little indentations to mark out where you will cut it into 12 equal pieces.
5. The neatest way of cutting the dough is to use unflavoured dental floss. Simply slide a long piece of floss under the roll of dough and align it with one of your cutting indentations, then cross the ends of the floss over each other and pull in opposite directions until you've made a clean cut through the roll. You can also use a knife or dough scraper to cut, but the rolls can get a bit squished when you cut the dough this way, and the chocolate may get messy.
6. Arrange the rolls swirl-side up on the prepared baking tray. Cover with an inverted tray of the same size or some loosely draped cling film (plastic wrap) and proof at room temperature for 45 minutes to 1 hour.
7. Preheat the oven to 180°C (350°F).
8. Pour the cream over the rolls and brush it evenly over the tops and sides. Sprinkle the hot chocolate powder over the top and spread it about with a spoon so it mixes in with the cream.
9. Bake for 28–32 minutes, or until the rolls are a light golden brown.
10. While the rolls are baking, you can prepare a chocolate drizzle for the top. This step is completely optional, as the rolls are chocolatey enough as they are! Scoop the chocolate spread into a small plastic bag or a reusable piping bag with a tiny nozzle. Seal it up and squish the chocolate around in the bag to soften it using the warmth of your hands. If using a plastic bag, just snip off the corner.
11. Remove the rolls from the oven and pipe a diagonal zig-zag of the chocolate spread over the top, then sprinkle with chopped hazelnuts, if desired.
12. These are best enjoyed warm from the oven. Store any leftover rolls in the fridge for up to 3 days and reheat in the microwave for 25–30 seconds to make them squidgy and melty again.

Pizza

3

Pizza has a piece of my heart. I challenge you to name a food more joy-inducing and universally loved than pizza.

Its brilliance lies in its simplicity; it's made of dough, sauce, cheese and a few humble toppings, but the result of these baked together is nothing short of extraordinary.

Pizza is comforting, fun to share and completely customisable. You can get creative and come up with new topping combinations using seasonal ingredients, or simply fall back on classic flavour combos that have been enjoyed for centuries. There is no right or wrong way to top your pizza.

My goal with this chapter is to inspire you to make pizza at home that will have you think twice before ordering it for delivery, because the truth is that you can make it just as well (or better!) at home.

Pizza dough is easy for beginners to master, but it does require a bit of hands-off proofing time to allow it to ferment, develop bubbles and become pliable enough to stretch out. Once it's portioned into dough balls, you can leave it at room temperature and ignore it for a few hours until it's time to top and bake your pizzas, or you can pop it in the refrigerator or freeze it to use later.

Of course, pizza isn't the only thing you can make with pizza dough. I'll show you how to turn this dough into Cheat's Ciabatta (page 172), Mini Calzones (page 160), Flatbreads (page 176), Pizza Sandwiches (pages 169-170), Fougasse (page 178) and ... wait for it ... Doughnuts (page 182)! And don't forget, you can make one batch of pizza dough and try multiple recipes in this chapter – super handy for those times you find yourself with a spare pizza dough ball and need some inspiration for what to do with it. But first, check out the 'Pizza Dough Must-knows' on page 134 to ensure that you're fully prepared to start working with this dough.

Pizza Dough
must-knows

FLOUR

White bread flour or 'Tipo 00' pizza flour are the best flours for making pizza dough due to their high gluten and protein content (around 12 per cent), which makes the dough nice and stretchy. You can use plain (all-purpose) flour, but reduce the water quantity to 350 ml (12 fl oz/scant 1½ cups) and only add more water if the dough is very dry. The results will always be better with bread flour or Tipo 00 pizza flour; the dough will be bubblier and easier to work with and stretch.

BAKING METHODS

There are many methods for baking pizza. Here I will explain each baking option, and you can choose to use the method that suits you and your kitchen set-up best. You can use any of these for any of the pizza recipes in this chapter.

FRYING PAN METHOD

I've outlined this method in detail on page 144. I believe this is the best way to bake pizza at home without a pizza oven. It involves cooking the base of the pizza dough in a frying pan until it's crispy before putting it under the grill (broiler) to finish. If this is tricky to visualise, there is a QR code for a video tutorial on page 138.

PIZZA OVEN

If you have a pizza oven or have plans to get one, be sure you read the instructions provided by the maker of the oven to achieve the best results for your exact model. Pizza ovens can get much hotter than domestic ovens, which means the pizzas will cook very quickly, usually within 90 seconds to 3 minutes. You'll need to preheat your pizza oven to around 370–425°C (700–800°F). You will need a pizza peel to transfer the pizza into the pizza oven and to rotate it if needed. Some pizza ovens do not include internal temperature gauges, so you may also need to invest in a digital infrared thermometer to read the temperature of the pizza oven before using it.

You may burn a few pizzas as you learn to use a pizza oven, but once you've nailed it, there is truly no baking method that compares. The extreme heat of the oven allows the crust to rise and crisp up to its full potential, and the flavour – particularly if using a wood-fired oven – is hard to beat.

PIZZA STONE/BAKING STEEL

Adding a pizza stone or baking steel to a normal oven during a long preheating session will increase the direct heat the dough is exposed to once it enters the oven, and this helps the dough to puff up and get crispy. Preheat your baking steel or pizza stone in the oven at the highest temperature possible (as close as you can get to 260°C/500°F) for at least 45 minutes, placing it on a rack in the upper third of the oven. A couple of minutes before putting the pizza into the oven, switch the oven to the grill (broiler) setting, if you have one. Using a pizza peel, transfer the pizza onto the pizza stone/ baking steel and bake under the grill for 2 minutes. Rotate the pizza 180 degrees so it can bake evenly, then switch the oven back to the normal setting at 260°C (500°F) for an additional 1–3 minutes. Watch it closely so the pizza doesn't burn. If your oven doesn't have an integrated grill (broiler), keep the oven on the normal setting and bake for 6–8 minutes, rotating halfway through.

OVEN

I find baking in the oven to be the most challenging, mostly because it can be difficult to achieve the heat that is needed to nicely crisp up the base of the pizza. A carbon steel pizza tray with vents at the bottom can help with this.

Set the oven temperature to the highest temperature possible (as close as you can get to 260°C/500°F) and bake the pizza on a pizza tray on an oven rack that has been placed in the lowest position. If you have a pizza setting on your oven, opt to use this, as it helps to ensure the base gets crispy. The baking time for each oven will vary, but it should range between 12 and 22 minutes. If the pizza base isn't getting crispy, place the tray directly on the bottom of the oven for the last few minutes of baking.

SPECIAL EQUIPMENT

LARGE FRYING PAN

If you'd like to try the frying pan method mentioned to the left, you will need a frying pan at least 30 cm (12 in) in diameter wide. This can be a large non-stick pan or a seasoned cast-iron pan, though I would avoid stainless steel as the dough may stick.

LARGE SPATULA OR FISH SLICE

If using the frying pan method, you'll need a large spatula (or my favourite, a fish slice) to transfer the pizza between the frying pan and the oven.

PIZZA PEEL

This is only necessary if you have a pizza oven or a baking steel/pizza stone, as it's the only way that you'll be able to transfer the uncooked pizza into the preheated oven. Always ensure the dough has been liberally floured before stretching and then scatter additional semolina onto the peel before pulling the pizza onto the peel. Give it a few shuffles to ensure the dough isn't stuck anywhere before you attempt to slide the pizza into your oven.

NON-STICK PIZZA TRAY

If you plan to bake your pizzas in the oven without a pizza stone or baking steel, I'd recommend investing in a carbon steel pizza tray. The air vents at the bottom help to encourage the base of the pizza to crisp up.

DOUGH TIMELINE

While the dough recipe for this chapter can be made from start to finish within about 3–3½ hours, I encourage you to also try the overnight or same-day methods explained on page 141. Not only does it give you a bit of flexibility for your timeline, but the secret ingredient of time can really benefit the pizza dough and its flavour and texture.

FREEZING PIZZA DOUGH

Pizza dough can be frozen right after the dough-ball shaping stage. Place each dough ball into individual freezer bags, then pop them into the freezer. The day before you plan to make your pizza, take a dough ball out of the freezer and place it, still in the freezer bag, in the refrigerator to thaw overnight. The next day, remove the dough ball from the bag, coat it in flour, place on a floured tray and cover with cling film (plastic wrap). Leave to proof at room temperature for about 2½–3 hours before using.

Topping Inspiration
for pizza, your way!

SAUCE

- One-minute Pizza Sauce (page 144)
- Fresh Basil Pesto (page 155)
- Perfect Pizza Sauce (page 161)
- Garlic Butter (page 146)
- extra virgin olive oil
- garlic oil
- white pizza sauce
- barbecue sauce
- no sauce (pizza bianca)

CHEESE

Chosen for their good meltability

- fresh mozzarella
- Fior di latte
- grated mozzarella
- provolone
- Parmesan
- Monterey Jack
- Gouda
- Gorgonzola
- Brie or Camembert
- fontina
- Taleggio

MEATY/PROTEIN TOPPINGS

- pepperoni
- salami
- bacon
- prosciutto (add after baking)
- sausage
- spicy chorizo
- steak
- 'nduja
- ham
- anchovies
- chicken
- barbecue chicken
- pulled pork
- fried egg

VEGGIE TOPPINGS

Always sauté or roast veggies beforehand so they don't release water as the pizza cooks

- (bell) peppers
- olives
- red onions
- mushrooms
- artichokes
- asparagus
- aubergine (eggplant)
- jalapeños
- roasted garlic
- spinach
- cherry tomatoes
- corn
- thinly sliced potatoes
- squash
- courgette (zucchini)
- pumpkin

TO DRIZZLE

Drizzle on top once the pizza is out of the oven

- extra virgin olive oil
- garlic oil
- chilli oil
- Homemade Hot Honey (page 152)
- aged balsamic vinegar
- Chimichurri Sauce (page 36)
- Fresh Basil Pesto (page 155)

TO GARNISH

The finishing touches before serving

- fresh basil
- fresh oregano
- chilli flakes
- rocket (arugula) salad
- freshly grated Parmesan
- Pink Pickled Onions (page 90)
- toasted pumpkin seeds

Pizza Dough

MAKES 4 × 250 G (9 OZ) PIZZA DOUGH BALLS; EACH PIZZA DOUGH BALL YIELDS A 30 CM (12 IN) PIZZA

TIME: 3–3¼ HOURS, DEPENDING ON PROOFING TIMES

385 ml (13 fl oz/1½ cups) warm water (40–43°C/105–110°F)
4 g (1 teaspoon) instant yeast*
15 ml (1 tablespoon) extra virgin olive oil
5 g (1 teaspoon) honey, sugar or agave
600 g (1 lb 5 oz/4¾ cups) white bread flour or 'Tipo 00' pizza flour, plus extra for dusting
12 g (2¼ teaspoons) fine sea salt
fine semolina, for dusting (optional)

* If you are using active dry or fresh yeast, please see page 14.

Scan the QR code for a video tutorial to accompany the recipe!

stage 1

Mix & Stretch & Fold

1. In a large mixing bowl, whisk together the warm water, instant yeast, extra virgin olive oil and honey until combined. Tip in the bread flour and fine sea salt and stir with a spoon until a shaggy dough mixture has formed. If using a stand mixer, use the dough hook attachment for this step. Choose any method below to finish mixing the dough.

To finish mixing by hand:
Remove any rings, wash your hands and then squish together the dough with one hand for a minute or two until no dry patches remain and the dough has come together nicely. Remove any excess dough from your hand, then cover the bowl with a clean tea towel and leave to proof at room temperature for 15 minutes.

To finish mixing with a spoon:
If you'd rather not use your hand to mix the dough (some people don't like it!), then you can continue using a spoon. You'll need to stir the dough quite aggressively for a minute or two to ensure that it's well mixed and no dry patches remain. Cover the bowl with a clean tea towel and leave to proof at room temperature for 15 minutes.

To finish mixing with a stand mixer:
If using a stand mixer, continue mixing using the dough hook attachment at medium speed for about 1 minute. Scrape the dough away from the hook, cover the bowl with a clean tea towel and leave to proof at room temperature for 15 minutes.

2. After 15 minutes, it's time to stretch and fold. Dip your hand into a bowl of water before touching the dough to prevent it from sticking to your fingers. Now take hold of the edge of the dough at the 12 o'clock position. Pull it up slightly to stretch, then pull it down over the bulk of the dough, finishing in the 6 o'clock position. Repeat this action on all sides of the bowl until it feels like you've created tension and you're unable to stretch the dough up and over itself anymore. The dough should have tightened up into a rough ball.
3. Cover and proof at room temperature for another 15 minutes, then stretch and fold once more.

stage 2

Shaping into Dough Balls

4. Now it's time to shape the dough into balls if you intend to use it to make pizza. You'll notice that some of the recipes in this chapter require different-sized dough balls, so read the instructions for the recipe you're making and work out what size you need before you shape the dough.

5. Tip the dough out onto a floured work surface, but don't add any flour to the top of the dough. Using a dough scraper or sharp knife, cut the pizza dough into four 250 g (9 oz) portions. If you're making smaller pizzas for kids or people with smaller appetites, adjust the size of the dough balls to meet your requirements.

6. Take the first dough portion, flour your fingers and grab each side of the dough. Pull the edges slightly outwards, then bring them towards the centre of the dough ball, crossing them over each other. Repeat this on all sides until you're left with a tight dough ball shape. Flip the dough ball over and place it, seam-side down, on an un-floured section of work surface. Flour your hands and cup your palms around the dough ball. Gently move the dough ball around using your palms until it's smooth and round on all sides, then pick it up and pinch together the seam at the bottom to secure the shape (see my video tutorial if you need help with this). Repeat this process with the remaining dough balls.

7. Coat each dough ball with a mixture of flour and fine semolina (if you have it). Place them on a liberally floured tray measuring at least 23 × 33 cm (9 × 13 in) and cover with cling film (plastic wrap). Leave to proof at room temperature for at least 2–3 hours so they can puff up and become easy to stretch. They should have spread out and nearly doubled in size by the time they're ready. On cold days, this can take a bit longer; on warm days, it could take less time. Once the dough balls have finished proofing, you're ready to make your pizza.

Make it Ahead – Overnight Pizza Dough

1. If you're preparing the dough in advance, you'll need to place it in the refrigerator after the second set of stretch and folds instead of shaping it into dough balls immediately.
2. Cover the bowl tightly with cling film (plastic wrap) or transfer it into a lidded container that is big enough to allow the dough to rise a little. Refrigerate overnight, then remove the dough from the refrigerator and shape into dough balls as instructed in step 5. Leave to rest, covered with cling film, for about 2½–3 hours before making your pizza.

See page 135 for instructions on freezing pizza dough.

Make it Ahead – Same-Day Pizza Dough

You can also essentially pause the pizza dough process if you want to make it earlier on the day you plan to use it. After the second set of stretch and folds, cover the mixing bowl and place it in the refrigerator. Then, 2–3 hours before you plan to use the dough, remove from the refrigerator and continue as stated from step 5.

Stretching Pizza Dough

1. If you're new to stretching pizza dough, it may take a little practice to get the hang of it. You can scan the QR code on page 144 to see a video tutorial for my favourite method of stretching dough. I call it 'the steering wheel method', and it's great for beginners. First, liberally flour your work surface and place the pizza dough ball on top of the flour. Add a little flour to the top of the pizza dough ball, then start by pressing around the circumference of the dough to form the crust area or the handles of the 'steering wheel'.

2. Use both hands to pick up the dough ball from the top using the 'handles' you've just formed. Stretch and turn the dough as if you were turning a steering wheel, repositioning your hands to a different portion of the 'handles' after each little stretch. The weight of the dough hanging down should help the pizza dough to stretch out as you perform this motion.

3. Lay the semi-stretched dough on to the floured surface and then pick it up again, but this time slide your knuckles (both hands) under the centre of the dough. Gently pull your fists apart from one another to stretch out the dough. Reposition your fists under the dough and stretch them apart again. Repeat until the dough measures about 30 cm (12 in) across, with the crust area remaining slightly thicker than the rest of the dough.

Frying Pan Margherita Pizza with One-minute Pizza Sauce

Let's start with a classic margherita pizza to demonstrate my favourite method for baking pizza at home without a pizza oven. The frying pan method helps to achieve a crispy, golden base, and the extreme heat from the grill (broiler) allows the pizza to bake in a matter of minutes.

MAKES 1 × 30 CM (12 IN) PIZZA

extra virgin olive oil, for drizzling
250 g (9 oz) Pizza Dough ball (page 138), fully proofed
plain (all-purpose) or bread flour, for dusting
100 g (3½ oz/scant ½ cup) One-minute Pizza Sauce (see below)
100 g (3½ oz) fresh mozzarella or fior di latte, torn
6 fresh basil leaves
1 tablespoon grated Parmesan or vegetarian Italian-style hard cheese

1. Preheat the grill (broiler) in your oven to high (275°C/525°F) and position the rack in the top third of the oven.
2. Drizzle a little extra virgin olive oil into a large non-stick or cast-iron frying pan (30 cm/12 in or larger) and heat over a medium–high heat.
3. Once the frying pan is nice and hot, stretch out your pizza dough following the method on page 142.
4. Lay the stretched-out dough out on the preheated frying pan. While the base of the dough is crisping up, spread the pizza sauce over the surface. Dot the mozzarella over the top, followed by the fresh basil leaves, then drizzle with olive oil.
5. After about 4 minutes, when the base of the pizza is golden brown and crispy, use a large spatula to transfer the pizza to under the grill (broiler). The grill will be very hot and the pizza should only take about 3–4 minutes to finish baking. If it fits, and your pan is ovenproof, you can simply transfer your frying pan into the oven without removing the pizza.
6. When the pizza is ready, top it with additional fresh basil leaves, a scattering of freshly grated Parmesan and a final drizzle of extra virgin olive oil, then cut into slices and enjoy immediately.

One-minute Pizza Sauce

MAKES ENOUGH FOR 4 × 30 CM (12-INCH) PIZZAS (400 G/ 14 OZ/1¾ CUPS)

400 g (14 oz) tin good-quality crushed tomatoes
2 teaspoons extra virgin olive oil
¼ teaspoon garlic granules
¼ teaspoon flaky sea salt
few pinches of dried herbs, such as basil and oregano (optional)

1. Simply mix all the ingredients together and use as instructed.
2. Store any leftover sauce in a sealed container in the refrigerator and use within 5 days. Alternatively, it can be frozen in a zip-top freezer bag and thawed in the fridge overnight before using the following day.

TIP:

See page 136 for topping inspiration so you can customise your own frying pan pizza.

Scan the QR code for a video tutorial to accompany the recipe!

Cheesy Garlic Pizza Bread

The sizzle of the garlic butter on this cheesy garlic pizza bread has hooked over 75 million people into watching the 'Marinated Tomato and Burrata Pizza' video on my social media channels. Plenty of commenters mentioned that they'd prefer to eat the cheesy garlic pizza bread without any of the extra toppings, and I wholeheartedly endorse this! It makes for a delicious side dish, but it also acts as the base for a few other pizzas in this chapter.

MAKES 1 CHEESY GARLIC PIZZA BREAD, SERVES 3–4 AS A SIDE

extra virgin olive oil, for drizzling
250 g (9 oz) Pizza Dough ball (page 138), fully proofed
1 batch Garlic Butter (see below)
70 g (2¼ oz/¾ cup) grated mozzarella
40 g (1½ oz/scant ½ cup) Parmesan or vegetarian Italian-style hard cheese, grated

1. Preheat the grill (broiler) in your oven to high (275°C/525°F) and position the rack in the top third of the oven.
2. Drizzle a little extra virgin olive oil into a large non-stick or cast-iron frying pan (30 cm/12 in or larger) and heat over a medium–high heat. Stretch the pizza dough out to a 30 cm (12 in) round (see page 142) and carefully lay it into the pan.
3. As the dough is cooking, brush the entire surface of the dough (including the crust) with the garlic butter. Sprinkle the grated mozzarella and Parmesan over the top.
4. After about 4 minutes, when the bottom of the crust is golden and crispy, use a large spatula to transfer the pizza to under the grill (broiler). The grill should finish cooking the top of the base in about 2–4 minutes, but watch it closely so it doesn't burn.
5. The garlic bread is ready once the garlic butter is sizzling and the cheese is starting to turn golden brown in places. Cut into slices and enjoy immediately. Allow to cool for a few minutes before devouring warm with those you love! If you find yourself with leftovers, just wrap them tightly in cling film (plastic wrap) and store in the refrigerator for up to 2 days. Microwave for 15–20 seconds to bring them back to life before enjoying.

Garlic Butter

MAKES 5 TABLESPOONS (75 G)

1½ tablespoons salted butter
1½ tablespoons extra virgin olive oil
4 garlic cloves, minced
1 tablespoon flat-leaf parsley, finely chopped

1. In a small frying pan over a medium–low heat, gently melt the butter with the extra virgin olive oil and minced garlic.
2. Stir to combine, then reduce the heat to low and simmer for 1–2 minutes. Stir in the chopped parsley, then remove from the heat and set aside until ready to use. Kept in the refrigerator, this will last up to 5 days.

TOPPING TIP:

Use this pizza bread as the base for the Marinated Tomato & Burrata Pizza (page 148) or the Lemony Salad Pizza (page 151).

Marinated Tomato & Burrata Pizza

A cheesy garlic pizza bread base topped with flavourful marinated tomatoes and creamy burrata. This is one of my most popular recipes, and is best enjoyed al fresco when the sun is shining and the tomatoes are at their peak! Everyone I've made this for goes wild for it, and my son has declared it is his favourite food in the world.

MAKES 1 × 30 CM (12 IN) PIZZA

1 Cheesy Garlic Pizza Bread, baked (page 146)
1 batch Marinated Tomatoes (see below)
150 g (5 oz) ball burrata or dollops of Homemade Stracciatella (page 70)
garlic oil, for drizzling
dried chilli flakes (optional)
flaky sea salt and freshly ground black pepper

1. Make the Cheesy Garlic Pizza Bread following the recipe on page 146. When the base is out of the oven, immediately spoon the marinated tomatoes over the top.
2. Place the ball of burrata in the middle of the pizza and drizzle it with a little garlic olive oil. Finish with a pinch of flaky sea salt and some freshly ground pepper, along with some dried chilli flakes, if using, and serve immediately.

Marinated Tomatoes

250 g (9 oz) cherry tomatoes, quartered
2 tablespoons extra virgin olive oil
1 teaspoon balsamic vinegar
1–2 garlic cloves, minced
3 tablespoons finely sliced fresh basil
flaky sea salt and freshly ground black pepper

1. Combine all the ingredients in a bowl and season with flaky sea salt and freshly ground black pepper. Set aside to marinate for at least 20 minutes before using. You can prepare the tomatoes up to a day in advance and store them in a sealed container in the fridge until you need them.
2. If you're using them for the recipe above, drain any excess liquid away from the tomatoes before adding them to the pizza, and reserve it as a sauce for dipping your crusts into later.

TOPPING TIP:

Top crostini with these tasty tomatoes for a delicious bruschetta appetiser, or add a spoonful to a sandwich to kick the flavour up a notch.

Lemony Salad Pizza

This pizza was inspired by a crisp, summery Caesar salad. The cheesy, garlicky pizza base acts as one big crouton, and it's perfectly balanced by the light, zesty salad on top. I have a feeling you'll want to pile all your salads on top of a pizza base after you try this one ...

MAKES 1 × 30 CM (12 IN) PIZZA

1 Cheesy Garlic Pizza Bread (page 146)

FOR THE LEMONY SALAD
½ head romaine lettuce, chopped
handful of rocket (arugula)
2 tablespoons extra virgin olive oil
2 teaspoons lemon juice
3 tablespoons grated Parmesan or vegetarian Italian-style hard cheese, plus extra to serve
flaky sea salt and freshly ground black pepper

FOR THE GARLICKY BREADCRUMBS
handful of breadcrumbs, homemade or store-bought
1 tablespoon Garlic Butter (page 146) (see note below)

* When making the garlic butter for the Cheesy Garlic Pizza Bread, add an extra ½ tablespoon butter and an extra ½ tablespoon olive oil to increase the quantity, then reserve 1 tablespoon of the garlic butter to use here.

1. To make the salad, combine all the ingredients in a large bowl and toss together. Set aside.
2. For the garlicky breadcrumbs, tip the breadcrumbs into a frying pan with the garlic butter and sauté over a medium heat for 3–4 minutes until golden brown and crispy. Transfer to plate lined with a paper towel to absorb any excess oil.
3. Make the Cheesy Garlic Pizza Bread following the recipe on page 146. When the base is out of the oven, top it with the lemony salad. Sprinkle the garlicky breadcrumbs over the top and finish with some more grated Parmesan and some freshly ground black pepper to taste. Slice and enjoy immediately.

Spicy Pepperoni Pizza with Hot Honey

This pizza ticks all the flavour boxes for me: salty, spicy and sweet. If you've never tried hot honey on a pizza, now is the time. The quantities stated are for guidance only – I encourage you to measure the cheese, pepperoni and pickled jalapeños with your heart. Who am I to tell you how much cheese you should be using?!

MAKES 1 × 30 CM (12 IN) PIZZA

extra virgin olive oil, for drizzling
250 g (9 oz) Pizza Dough ball (page 138), fully proofed
100 g (3½ oz/scant ½ cup) One-minute Pizza Sauce (page 144) or Perfect Pizza Sauce (page 161)
100 g (3½ oz/1 cup) fresh mozzarella or grated mozzarella
50 g (8–12 slices/2 oz) spicy pepperoni, spicy salami or spicy chorizo
12 pickled jalapeño slices

TO GARNISH
6 fresh basil leaves
finely grated Parmesan
Homemade Hot Honey (see right), for drizzling

1. Preheat the grill (broiler) in your oven to high (275°C/525°F) and position the rack in the top third of the oven.
2. Drizzle a little extra virgin olive oil into a large non-stick or cast-iron frying pan (30 cm/12 in or larger) and heat over a medium–high heat. Stretch the pizza dough out to a 30 cm (12 in) round (page 142) and carefully lay it into the pan.
3. As the dough is cooking, top with the pizza sauce, cheese, pepperoni and pickled jalapeños.
4. After 4 minutes, or when the base of the pizza is crispy and golden brown, use a large spatula to transfer it to under the grill (broiler). Cook under the direct heat for 2–4 minutes, or until the crust and pepperoni are crisping up and the cheese has melted.
5. When the pizza is ready, garnish with fresh basil leaves, a dusting of grated Parmesan and a good drizzle of hot honey, then serve.

Homemade Hot Honey

MAKES 340 G (12 OZ/1 CUP)

340 g (12 oz/1 cup) runny honey
1½ tablespoons dried chilli flakes
2 teaspoons apple cider vinegar

1. In a small saucepan over a medium heat, bring the honey and dried chilli flakes to a simmer. Simmer for 1 minute, then remove from the heat and stir in the apple cider vinegar.
2. Pour the hot honey into a sterilised glass jar with a lid and store at room temperature for up to 2 months.

TIP:

As with all the pizzas in this chapter, please feel free to use any of the baking methods listed on page 134 if you'd prefer them to the frying pan method.

Roasted Pumpkin Pizza with Fresh Basil Pesto

This pizza is a celebration of autumnal flavours. Roasted pumpkin, nutty toasted pumpkin seeds and creamy ricotta are balanced out by a little punch of acidity from pink pickled onions and bright green basil pesto. If you don't have fresh pumpkin readily available, cubes of butternut squash make an excellent substitute.

125 g (4 oz/1 cup) pumpkin or
  butternut squash, cubed
extra virgin olive oil, for
  drizzling
1 tablespoon pumpkin seeds
115 g (3¾ oz/½ cup) ricotta
  cheese
**250 g (9 oz) Pizza Dough ball
  (page 138), fully proofed**
2 tablespoons Fresh Basil
  Pesto (see below) or
  store-bought
2½ tablespoons Pink Pickled
  Onions (page 90)
flaky sea salt and freshly
  ground black pepper

1. Preheat the oven to 190°C (375°F).
2. On a baking tray, toss the pumpkin (or butternut squash) cubes with a drizzle of olive oil and a sprinkle of salt and pepper. Push them up to make a little room, then add the pumpkin seeds to the space you've created. Rub them with a tiny bit of olive oil and sprinkle with a little flaky sea salt. Bake for 15–20 minutes until the pumpkin cubes are tender and starting to char around the edges, and the pumpkin seeds are toasty and crispy.
3. Remove the tray from the oven, then preheat the grill (broiler) in your oven to high (275°C/525°F) and position the rack in the top third of the oven.
4. In a bowl, mix the ricotta cheese with a pinch of salt and pepper and set aside.
5. Drizzle a little extra virgin olive oil into a large non-stick or cast-iron frying pan (30 cm/12 in or larger) and heat over a medium–high heat. Stretch the pizza dough out to a 30 cm (12 in) round (page 142) and carefully lay it into the pan.
6. As the dough is cooking, top it with the ricotta cheese and cubes of roasted pumpkin.
7. After 4 minutes, or when the base of the pizza is crispy and brown, use a large spatula to transfer it from the frying pan to under the grill (broiler). Let it cook under the direct heat for about 3–5 minutes, or until the crust is cooked to your liking.
8. When the pizza is ready, dollop the fresh pesto over the top and scatter with a few pink pickled onions before finishing with the crispy pumpkin seeds. Slice and serve.

Fresh Basil Pesto

**MAKES 200 G
(7 OZ/GENEROUS
¼ CUP)**

2 garlic cloves, minced
12 g (½ oz/4 teaspoons)
  finely chopped pine nuts,
  pistachios or walnuts
2 pinches of flaky sea salt
60 g (2 oz/2 heaping cups)
  fresh basil leaves, stems
  removed
75 ml (5 tablespoons)
  extra virgin olive oil
40 g (1½ oz)/6 tablespoons
  Parmesan or vegetarian
  Italian-style hard cheese,
  grated
small squeeze of lemon
  juice (optional)

1. Add the garlic, pine nuts and salt to the bowl of a food processor. Pulse until the pine nuts are roughly chopped. Add the basil and half the olive oil and pulse until the basil is finely chopped.
2. Drizzle the rest of olive oil into the basil mixture while continuing to pulse until the pesto has emulsified. Stir in the grated Parmesan. If you like a zingier pesto, try stirring in a squeeze of lemon juice at the end.
3. This recipe makes more pesto than is needed for the pizza. Store excess pesto in the fridge in a small, lidded container – the less air in the container, the better. It is best used within 3–4 days.

TOPPING TIP:

You can use leftover pesto from this recipe to make a Pesto Chicken Melt (page 98) or the Caprese Pizza Sandwich (page 170). Alternatively, use it as a dip for a warm batch of Garlic Butter Breadsticks (page 180).

Roasted Pepper & Chimichurri Pizza

You can probably imagine how much pizza my family consumed during the recipe-testing phase of this book. The answer is ... A LOT! This pizza received very high praise from my husband and son, so the recipe instantly won a spot in the book. My daughter Sophie refused to taste it, but she's a plain cheese pizza kind of gal, so who can blame her? Chimichurri and pizza may not seem the most likely of pairings, but I promise that once you taste it, you will understand ... and maybe one day my daughter will too.

MAKES 1 × 30 CM (12 IN) PIZZA

½ red (bell) pepper, chopped
½ yellow (bell) pepper, chopped
1 small red onion (½ large), chopped
extra virgin olive oil, for drizzling
250 g (9 oz) Pizza Dough ball (page 138), fully proofed
100 g (3½ oz/1 cup) grated mozzarella
3–4 tablespoons Chimichurri Sauce (page 36)
flaky sea salt and freshly ground black pepper

1. Begin by roasting or sautéing the peppers and onion. If roasting, preheat the oven to 200°C (400°F). Toss the peppers and onion in a little extra virgin olive oil on a small baking tray and season with salt and pepper. Bake for 20–25 minutes, or until the peppers are soft, sweet and starting to char on the edges. If sautéing, heat a drizzle of olive oil in a medium-sized frying pan over a medium–high heat. Add the peppers and onion, season with salt and pepper, and sauté for about 10 minutes, or until the peppers have softened. Set aside.
2. Preheat the grill (broiler) in your oven to high (275°C/525°F) and position the rack in the top third of the oven.
3. Drizzle a little extra virgin olive oil into a large non-stick or cast-iron frying pan (30 cm/12 in or larger) and heat over a medium–high heat. Stretch the pizza dough out to a 30 cm (12 in) round (page 142) and carefully lay it into the pan.
4. As the base is cooking, sprinkle the cheese over the dough, then spoon the peppers and onion into an even layer on top.
5. After 4 minutes, or when the base of the pizza is crispy and golden brown, use a large spatula to transfer it to under the grill (broiler). Leave the pizza to cook under the direct heat for 2–4 minutes, or until the crust is crisping up and the cheese has melted.
6. When the pizza is ready, spoon some Chimichurri Sauce over the peppers, onion and cheese, and brush some over the crust, too. Slice and serve.

TOPPING TIP:

To make this pizza extra indulgent, add some slices of grilled steak once it's out of the oven.

Stuffed Crust Pizza

As if pizza wasn't already cheesy enough! If you're one to normally leave the crusts on the plate, I have a feeling you may change your ways when the crusts are filled with oozy, melty cheese.

MAKES 1 × 25 CM (10 IN) PIZZA

extra virgin olive oil, for drizzling

plain (all-purpose) or bread flour, for dusting

250 g (9 oz) Pizza Dough ball (page 138), fully proofed

250 g (9 oz/2½ cups) grated mozzarella

80 g (2¾ oz/⅓ cup) Perfect Pizza Sauce (page 161) or One-minute Pizza Sauce (page 144)

toppings of your choice (see page 136 for inspiration)

½ batch Garlic Butter (page 146), for brushing (optional)

1. Preheat the oven to 240°C (465°F) and place the oven rack into the lowest position. Line a large baking tray (33 × 46 cm/13 × 18 in) with non-stick baking parchment and spread a little olive oil on the paper.

2. With floured hands, place the pizza dough ball on the oiled baking parchment and stretch it out, pulling the dough towards the edges of the tray to ensure it is as thin as possible – you want the edges to be as thin as the rest of the dough.

3. Arrange half of the grated mozzarella around the edges of the dough, then fold the edges of the dough over the cheese and press down to seal the cheese inside. You should have a thin middle section of base encircled by a thicker mound of cheese-stuffed dough. Sprinkle a little extra mozzarella around the perimeter of the dough if you'd like some toasty, crispy cheese baked on top of the crust.

4. Par-bake the crust for 10 minutes and then remove from the oven. Add the sauce, the remaining mozzarella and your toppings of choice.

5. Continue baking the pizza for an additional 10–15 minutes, or until the crust is a light golden brown and the base is crispy. If you notice the base is not crisping up, place the tray directly on the bottom of the oven for the final 3–5 minutes.

6. This is completely optional, but try brushing some Garlic Butter (page 146) over the cheese-stuffed-crusts before serving – I promise you won't regret it!

Spinach & Ricotta Mini Calzones with Perfect Pizza Sauce

These flavour-packed pizza parcels can be stuffed with anything your heart desires! Here, they're packed with a deliciously cheesy spinach and ricotta filling, and are paired with a warm pizza sauce for dipping. Swap out the spinach for some salami, ham or cooked sausage if you'd prefer a meatier calzone ...

**MAKES 8 MINI
CALZONES**

500 g (1 lb 2 oz) Pizza Dough
   (page 138)
plain (all-purpose) or bread
   flour, for dusting
1 batch Perfect Pizza Sauce
   (see below), to serve
20g (¾ oz) Parmesan, grated,
   for sprinkling over before
   baking

FOR THE FILLING
½ tablespoon extra virgin
   olive oil, plus extra for
   drizzling
250 g (9 oz) baby spinach
   leaves
3 garlic cloves, minced
¼ teaspoon flaky sea salt
250 g (9 oz/generous 1 cup)
   ricotta, drained
100 g (3½ oz/1 cup) grated
   mozzarella
30 g (1 oz/¼ cup) Parmesan,
   grated,
zest of ½ lemon
freshly ground black pepper

FOR THE EGG WASH
1 egg, whisked
1 tablespoon water

1. Prepare the pizza dough up to step 4 on page 140. You'll need 500 g (1 lb 2 oz) of the dough for this recipe; save the rest to use in another recipe like Cheat's Ciabatta (page 172), Fougasse (page 178), Breadsticks (page 180) or Doughnuts (page 182).
2. Flour your work surface and cut your dough into 8 equal portions (62 g/2¼ oz each) and shape them into dough balls (see steps 4–7, page 140). Place the dough balls on a tray, cover them with cling film (plastic wrap) and leave to proof at room temperature for 1½–2 hours.
3. Make the spinach and ricotta filling. Heat the olive oil in a large frying pan over a medium–high heat. Add the spinach and stir to coat it in the olive oil. Reduce the heat to medium and cook for 2 minutes, then add the garlic and salt and cook for another 2 minutes. Remove from the heat and set aside to cool slightly.
4. In a medium bowl, mix together the ricotta, mozzarella, Parmesan and lemon zest. Season with black pepper.
5. Place the cooked spinach into a fine-mesh sieve and squeeze to remove any excess liquid. Chop, then add the spinach to the ricotta mixture and stir until evenly combined. Taste for seasoning and adjust if needed.
6. Preheat the oven to 230°C (450°F) and place the oven rack in the lowest position. Line a large baking tray (33 × 46 cm/13 × 18 in) with non-stick baking parchment and spread a little olive oil on the paper.
7. Lightly flour your work surface and press or roll one of the dough balls into a 15 cm (6 in) round. Spoon 60 g (2 oz/¼ cup) of the spinach mixture on to the bottom half of the round, then fold the top half of the dough over to form a half-moon shape. Press the edges of the dough together to seal, then crimp the edge with a fork. Place on the prepared baking tray and repeat the process with the remaining dough balls and filling.
8. In a small bowl, whisk together the egg wash ingredients. Lightly brush the egg wash over each of the mini calzones, then use kitchen shears or a sharp knife to slice two little air vents into the top of each one. These will help to prevent them from bursting open. Sprinkle the Parmesan over the tops of each and then bake for 20–25 minutes, or until golden brown and crispy on their tops and bottoms.
9. Transfer the calzones to a cooling rack for a few minutes, then serve warm alongside little bowls of warm pizza sauce for dunking.

Perfect Pizza Sauce

MAKES 400 G (14 OZ/1¼ CUPS)

1½ tablespoons extra virgin olive oil
2 garlic cloves, minced
½ teaspoon Italian dried herbs or
   dried oregano (optional)
pinch of dried chilli flakes (optional)
400 g (14 oz) tin crushed tomatoes
½ teaspoon flaky sea salt
1–2 pinches granulated sugar
1 tablespoon finely chopped fresh
   basil leaves

1. This pizza sauce can be simmering away while you prepare the calzones. Heat the olive oil in a small saucepan over a medium heat, then add the garlic and bring to a simmer. Cook for about 1 minute, then add the dried herbs and/or chilli flakes, if using.
2. Add the tomatoes, salt and sugar. Bring the sauce to a gentle boil, then reduce the heat to low and simmer, uncovered, for about 10 minutes. Stir in the basil and continue simmering for another 10 minutes. Serve warm. Store any leftover sauce in a sealed container in the fridge for up to 5 days.

Zucchini Flatbread Pizza with Lemon Pistachio Pesto

We spend our summers in Sonoma County, California, visiting my family, soaking up the sunshine. My dad's impressive homegrown squash prompted me to create this summery flatbread pizza with grilled zucchini, burrata, preserved lemons and a lemon pistachio pesto. With so many interesting flavours and textures, this pizza is a must-try!

**MAKES 1 LARGE
THIN-CRUST PIZZA**

2 medium courgettes
  (zucchini), cut into long,
  thin strips
extra virgin olive oil, for
  drizzling
250 g (9 oz) Pizza Dough ball
  (page 138), fully proofed
150 g (5 oz) ball burrata or
  dollops of Homemade
  Stracciatella (page 70)
1 batch Lemon Pistachio
  Pesto (see below)
2 small preserved lemons,
  seeds removed, sliced into
  thin half-moons
1½ tablespoons shelled
  roasted and salted
  pistachios, very finely
  chopped
flaky sea salt and freshly
  ground black pepper

TO GARNISH
fresh basil leaves
lemon zest

TOPPING TIP:

Swap the courgette for
a couple of bunches
of grilled asparagus to
transform this into a
springtime pizza.

1. Preheat the oven to 240°C (465°F) and place the oven rack in the lowest position in the oven.
2. Lightly coat the courgette strips with olive oil and season with salt and pepper. Heat a large frying pan over a medium–high heat, and cook the strips for about 2–3 minutes on each side, or until both sides are slightly charred. Depending on the size of your frying pan, you may need to do this in batches.
3. Line a large tray (33 × 46 cm/13 × 18 in) with non-stick baking parchment. Brush some olive oil onto the parchment. Place the pizza dough ball into the centre of the tray, drizzle some olive oil over the top of it, and gently stretch each side of the dough out towards the edges of the tray. It won't reach to the very edges, but do try to stretch it as far as it will go – it should be very thin all over.
4. Par-bake the pizza base for 10–12 minutes, then remove from the oven and arrange the courgette strips on top as artfully as you can. Return to the oven to continue baking for another 6–8 minutes, or until the crust is a deep golden brown. If the bottom of the base hasn't crisped up at this point, place the tray directly on the base of the oven for a few extra minutes to blast it with direct heat. The crispiness is essential for this pizza.
5. Once the pizza is out of the oven, tear open the burrata and dot it evenly across the top. Give the pesto a stir and spoon it over the top of the burrata and on to the courgette strips. Nestle the sliced preserved lemons onto the pizza, then sprinkle over the finely chopped pistachios. Garnish with basil leaves and lemon zest, and season with one last sprinkle of salt and pepper.
6. Cut into squares and enjoy with a glass of something cold and refreshing in the sunshine!

Lemon Pistachio Pesto

**MAKES 50G (2 OZ/
SCANT ¼ CUP)**

2 tablespoons very finely
  chopped fresh basil
1 tablespoon shelled
  roasted and salted
  pistachios, very finely
  chopped
½ teaspoon lemon zest
1 teaspoon lemon juice
3 tablespoons extra
  virgin olive oil
¼ teaspoon flaky sea salt

1. Simply stir together all the ingredients in a small bowl. Taste for seasoning and adjust if needed.
2. Set aside until it's time to use. You can make the pesto a few hours in advance and store in a sealed container in the fridge, but the basil will brown over time so it's best used on the same day.

Potato & Rosemary Flatbread Pizza

The day I was testing this recipe, we had two workmen installing some boards in the loft space of our new house. They agreed to be honorary taste-testers for the day, and happily tried a few variations of this pizza. They dubbed this version the winner, and I totally agreed with them. If you're not a big fan of rosemary, you can sub in some chives, spring onions (scallions) or fresh thyme for an equally delicious result.

**MAKES 1 LARGE
THIN-CRUST PIZZA**

2 small red onions
(or 1 medium), sliced into
thin rings
2 teaspoons extra virgin
olive oil, plus extra for
drizzling
¼ teaspoon flaky sea salt
250 g (9 oz) Pizza Dough ball
(page 138), fully proofed
100 g (3½ oz/1 cup) grated
mozzarella
1 teaspoon finely chopped
fresh rosemary
1 small baking potato, very
thinly sliced using a sharp
knife or mandoline
freshly ground black pepper

1. Preheat the oven to 240°C (465°F) and place the oven rack in the lowest position in the oven.
2. Separate out the onion rings, and toss in a bowl with the olive oil, flaky sea salt and some freshly ground black pepper.
3. Line a large tray (33 × 46 cm/13 × 18 in) with non-stick baking parchment. Brush some olive oil onto the parchment. Place the pizza dough ball into the centre of the tray, drizzle some olive oil over the top of it, and gently stretch each side of the dough out towards the edges of the tray. It won't reach to the very edges, but do try to stretch it as far as it will go – it should be very thin all over.
4. Sprinkle the mozzarella over the dough and then scatter about two-thirds of the onions over the cheese. Sprinkle most of the rosemary over the top, but reserve a few pinches for later.
5. Arrange the potatoes in a single layer over the cheese and onions. They should cover the entire surface, so the cheese and onions aren't peeking through. Drizzle with olive oil and sprinkle with salt and pepper. Arrange the remaining onions over the top.
6. Bake for 24–28 minutes, or until the crust is a deep golden brown and super crispy all over. I recommend using a spatula to carefully lift and check the base of the pizza after around 24 minutes; if it isn't yet golden brown and crispy, transfer the tray directly to the base of the oven. The direct heat will help crisp it up in the final few minutes of baking.
7. Once the pizza is out of the oven, sprinkle the remaining rosemary over the top, then cut into squares and enjoy!

TOPPING TIP:

Omit the cheese and
red onions to make
a tasty potato and
rosemary flatbread.

Pizzetta Three Ways

Each pizza dough ball can be divided to create three delicious, crispy, mini pizzas. It was important to me to include a fruit-topped recipe in this chapter, but I couldn't decide on my favourite... so I'm sharing a trio of fruit pizza recipes so you can try them all!

MAKES 3 PIZZETTA

FOR THE BASES

250 g (9 oz) Pizza Dough (page 138), divided into three 83 g (3 oz) balls when shaping

extra virgin olive oil, for drizzling

CHOOSE YOUR PIZZETTA:

FOR THE BACON, DATE AND BRIE PIZZETTA

6 rashers smoked streaky bacon

6–9 small dates, cut into small bite-sized pieces

90 g (3 oz) Brie or Camembert cheese, torn

small handful of rocket (arugula), to garnish

balsamic vinegar, for drizzling

flaky sea salt

FOR THE BALSAMIC STRAWBERRY PIZZETTA (V)

225 g (8 oz/scant 1 cup) ricotta

1½ teaspoons honey

pinch of lemon zest, plus extra to serve

6–9 strawberries, sliced

9 fresh basil leaves, julienned

aged balsamic vinegar or balsamic glaze, for drizzling

FOR THE PEACH AND PROSCIUTTO PIZZETTA

1½ small peaches or nectarines, sliced

90 g (3 oz/scant 1 cup) grated mozzarella

3–6 slices prosciutto

9 fresh basil leaves, julienned

aged balsamic vinegar or balsamic glaze, for drizzling

TOPPING TIP:

If you have some Pink Pickled Onions (page 90) in the fridge, try adding a few to the Bacon, Date and Brie Pizzetta.

---

1. Make the pizza dough following the instructions on page 138. When you reach step 4, divide one of the normal 250 g (9 oz) portions of dough into three pieces. Shape these into smaller dough balls. Cover with a clean tea towel and leave to proof at room temperature for about 2–2½ hours.

2. When the dough has fully proofed, preheat the oven to 240°C (465°F) and place the oven rack in the lowest position in the oven.

3. Line a large tray (33 × 46 cm/13 × 18 in) with non-stick baking parchment. Brush some olive oil onto the parchment. Place one pizza dough ball onto the tray and stretch it out until nice and thin – it should make a long oval shape about 20 cm (8 in) long. Repeat with the other two dough balls, spacing them out evenly on the tray.

4. The timings for when you'll add the toppings to the pizzetta will vary. With some, you'll bake the toppings on the dough from the start. For others, you'll bake the dough as a flatbread and add the toppings at the end.

For the Bacon, Date and Brie Pizzetta, you'll need to prepare the bacon first. Cook it for 3–4 minutes in a small frying pan over a medium–high heat until partly cooked, or microwave on a small plate with a paper towel placed over the top for 1½ minutes. Chop the bacon into small pieces and sprinkle it over the bases – the bacon will finish crisping up in the oven. Add the chopped dates and dot the Brie over the top. Bake for 15–18 minutes on the lowest rack in the oven or until the crust and bases are golden brown and crispy. Toss the rocket in a small bowl with a dash of balsamic vinegar, a drizzle of extra virgin olive oil and a pinch of salt. Scatter the greens over the top of the pizzetta before serving.

For the Balsamic Strawberry Pizzetta, drizzle the dough with a little extra virgin olive oil and then bake it on the lowest rack in the oven without any toppings for about 14–16 minutes. While baking, stir together the ricotta, honey and lemon zest in a bowl. Slice the strawberries and basil. Once the pizzetta bases are golden and crispy, spread the ricotta mixture onto them and arrange the strawberries on top. Scatter over the julienned basil, a little more lemon zest and finish with a drizzle of aged balsamic vinegar and extra virgin olive oil.

For the Peach and Prosciutto Pizzetta, drizzle the dough with a little extra virgin olive oil and bake it on the lowest rack in the oven without any toppings for about 10 minutes. While the bases are baking, drizzle some olive oil into a preheated frying pan over a medium–high heat and fry the peaches for 2 minutes on each side until they've softened and charred. After 10 minutes, add the cheese to the bases and continue baking for another 6 minutes. When the pizzetta are out of the oven, arrange the peaches and prosciutto on top. Scatter over the julienned basil and finish with a drizzle of extra virgin olive oil and aged balsamic vinegar.

Mortadella Pizza Sandwich with Lemon Pistachio Pesto

Mortadella, burrata and a zingy lemon pistachio pesto are layered into a pillowy pocket of pizza bread to create an impressive and indulgent sandwich.

MAKES 1 LARGE PIZZA SANDWICH TO SERVE 1–2, DEPENDING ON HOW HUNGRY YOU ARE

250 g (9 oz) Pizza Dough ball (page 138), fully proofed

plain (all-purpose) or bread flour, for dusting

extra virgin olive oil, for drizzling

2–3 tablespoons Lemon Pistachio Pesto (page 163) (if you prefer, you can use the Fresh Basil Pesto on page 155, or store-bought pesto)

4–6 slices mortadella

150 g (5 oz) ball burrata or fresh mozzarella, sliced

1½ tablespoons crushed shelled roasted and salted pistachios

lemon zest, to garnish

TOPPING TIP:

If you can't find mortadella, you can opt to use ham or prosciutto instead. To make it vegetarian, use ribbons of grilled courgette (zucchini) instead of the mortadella.

Oven method

1. Preheat the oven to 240°C (465°F) and place the rack in the lowest position in the oven. Line a baking tray with non-stick baking parchment.
2. Stretch the pizza dough ball into a 30 cm (12 in) round (see page 142) and lay it on a lightly floured work surface. Drizzle extra virgin olive oil over the entire surface of the pizza dough.
3. Fold the dough into a half moon shape (with the oil enclosed), then drizzle a little more oil over the top and transfer it to the prepared baking tray. Bake for 13–15 minutes, or until the pizza bread is puffy and crisp, and has turned a light golden-brown colour.

Frying pan method

1. Preheat the grill (broiler) in your oven to high (275°C/525°F) and position the rack in the top third of the oven.
2. Drizzle a little extra virgin olive oil into a large non-stick or cast-iron frying pan (30 cm/12 in or larger) and heat over a medium–high heat.
3. Stretch out and fold the pizza dough as described above, then place into the hot frying pan. Cook for 4 minutes until the bottom is golden brown, then use a spatula to transfer the pizza bread to under the grill (broiler). Bake for 3–4 minutes, or until the top of the bread is crispy and golden brown.

Filling the sandwich

1. Remove the cooked pizza bread from the oven or frying pan and peel back the top half to expose the steamy, soft interior.
2. Spread the upper and lower sections of the bread with your choice of pesto, then layer on slices of mortadella. Tear the burrata or mozzarella over the mortadella, then drizzle with some more pesto. Finish with a scattering of crushed pistachios and some freshly grated lemon zest, then squish the pizza sandwich back together, cut in half and enjoy!

Caprese Pizza Sandwich

I know I shouldn't play favourites, but ... I would choose this veggie version of the pizza sandwich – every. Single. Time. There is no doubt that the mortadella version on page 169 is completely delicious (do give it a try!), but for me, tomatoes, basil and burrata always steal the crown.

MAKES 1 LARGE PIZZA SANDWICH TO SERVE 1–2, DEPENDING ON HOW HUNGRY YOU ARE

250 g (9 oz) Pizza Dough ball (page 138), fully proofed
extra virgin olive oil, for drizzling
2–3 tablespoons Fresh Basil Pesto (page 155) or store-bought pesto
handful of rocket (arugula)
aged balsamic or balsamic glaze, for drizzling
150 g (5 oz) ball burrata or fresh mozzarella, sliced
flaky sea salt and freshly ground black pepper

FOR THE MARINATED TOMATOES AND ONIONS
200 g (7 oz) cherry tomatoes, quartered
½ small red onion, thinly sliced
1½ tablespoons extra virgin olive oil
1 teaspoon balsamic vinegar
1–2 garlic cloves, minced
3 tablespoons fresh basil, julienned, plus a few leaves to garnish
flaky sea salt and freshly ground black pepper

1. Mix together the ingredients for the marinated tomatoes and onions in a bowl. Season with salt and pepper and set aside to marinate for at least 20 minutes. You can prepare them up to a day in advance and store them in a sealed container in the fridge until you need them.
2. To make the pizza sandwich bread, follow steps 1–3 of your preferred method on page 169. Once the bread has finished baking, return to this recipe.
3. Remove the pizza bread from the oven and peel back the top half to expose the steamy, soft interior. Spread the upper and lower sections of the bread with the pesto, and add a handful of rocket to the bottom half of the bread. Drizzle some olive oil and balsamic over the top of the rocket and season with salt and pepper.
4. Tear the burrata or mozzarella over the greens, then spoon the marinated tomatoes and onions over the top, reserving most of the juices they've released in the bowl (see tip).
5. Top with some fresh basil leaves and finish with one last drizzle of aged balsamic vinegar. Squish the entire sandwich together, cut in half and enjoy with a stack of napkins – it's a messy one!

TOPPING TIP:

Try dipping the sandwich into the reserved liquid from the tomatoes between bites.

Cheat's Ciabatta

I call this Cheat's Ciabatta because it feels a bit too good to be true to be able to turn pizza dough into a crusty, airy ciabatta roll. Use this bread to make sandwiches, garlic bread, bruschetta, *pan con tomate* and more! If you like, you can make an entire batch of Pizza Dough into Cheat's Ciabatta; just be sure that you have a large enough tray to accommodate all the rolls, and if not then arrange them between two trays.

MAKES 1 × 25 CM (10 IN) CIABATTA ROLL

250 g (9 oz) Pizza Dough ball (page 138), fully proofed
plain (all-purpose) or bread flour, for dusting

1. Preheat the oven to 240°C (465°F) and place the oven rack in the lowest position.
2. Dust a small baking tray with some flour. Using floured hands, gently stretch the fully proofed pizza dough ball into an oval shape about 25 cm (10 in) long. Place it on the baking tray and bake for 14–16 minutes, or until the ciabatta is a light golden brown colour.
3. Once out of the oven, transfer to a cooling rack and wait at least 10 minutes before cutting into it.

TOPPING TIP:

To make this into cheesy garlic bread, make a batch of the Garlic Butter from page 146. After the ciabatta has baked, slice it lengthways, brush the butter onto it, add 25 g (¼ cup) grated Parmesan and 50 g (½ cup) grated mozzarella, then bake at 200°C (400°F) for 10–15 minutes.

The Ultimate Grinder Sandwich

If you're wondering what a grinder sandwich is, you're not alone – I only found out what it was when it went viral on social media a few years back. Grinder is the name that some people on the East Coast of the USA use to describe a hot, toasted submarine sandwich. Here, toasty garlic bread is piled high with your favourite deli meats, melted cheese, crispy salad and zingy pink pickled onions. I admit there are a lot of components that go into making this sandwich, but I promise it is completely worth it!

MAKES 1 LARGE SANDWICH TO SERVE 1–2, DEPENDING ON HOW HUNGRY YOU ARE

1 Cheat's Ciabatta roll (page 172)
1½ tablespoons Garlic Butter (page 146), plus extra to serve
3 slices provolone or mozzarella
handful of grated Parmesan
100 g (3½ oz) selection of your favourite deli meats: salami, spicy salami, pepperoni, smoked ham and sliced turkey
handful of grated mozzarella
2 large handfuls shredded iceberg lettuce
small handful of pepperoncini or pickled chillies, chopped
4 slices of tomato
2 tablespoons Pink Pickled Onions (page 90), or sliced red onion
flaky sea salt and freshly ground black pepper

FOR THE SALAD DRESSING

1½ tablespoons mayonnaise
1 tablespoon extra virgin olive oil
½ teaspoon red wine vinegar (or brine from pepperoncini or pickled onions)
½ teaspoon dried Italian herbs
¼ teaspoon Dijon mustard
1 tablespoon flat-leaf parsley, chopped

TOPPING TIP:

If you prefer, you can swap the Cheat's Ciabatta for a large Soft Sandwich Roll (page 72).

1. Preheat the oven to 200°C (400°F).

2. Cut the roll in half lengthways and dig out some of the excess bread from either side of the roll – this helps to accommodate lots of filling. The leftover bread can be enjoyed as a chef's perk or turned into croutons (page 106). Brush both cut sides of the bread with garlic butter, then place the slices of provolone on one half and sprinkle a third of the Parmesan over the other half. Lay your choice of deli meats over both halves, then sprinkle another third of the Parmesan over the top, along with the grated mozzarella. Bake for 8–12 minutes, or until the bread is getting crispy and the cheese has melted.

3. While the sandwich is baking, start prepping the salad. In a large bowl, whisk together the dressing ingredients until smooth and season with salt and pepper. Just before the sandwich halves are ready to come out of the oven, add the lettuce and chopped pepperoncini/pickled chillies to the bowl, and toss to combine.

4. Remove the sandwich halves from the oven. Add the salad and tomato slices to the bottom half and season with salt and pepper. Divide the Pink Pickled Onions between both halves, then squeeze both sides of the sandwich together. I like to brush a bit of extra garlic butter over the top of the sandwich and finish with one final dusting of finely grated Parmesan.

5. Tightly wrapping the sandwich in baking parchment before cutting it in half will help to prevent all the toppings from sliding out as you eat the sandwich – and it makes it feel like you bought it from a deli, too!

Flatbreads with Creamy Tzatziki Dip

These chewy, slightly charred flatbreads are ideal for mopping up sauces and dips, and they also make a fabulous thick wrap for kebabs, gyros or falafel. Here, I've paired the flatbread with one of my favourite dips: tzatziki. I fell in love with this dip years ago when visiting Santorini with my husband, and it's been on a firm rotation in my kitchen ever since.

**MAKES 6
FLATBREADS**

1 full batch of Pizza Dough
(page 138), shaped into
6 dough balls (165 g/5¾ oz
each)
plain (all-purpose) or bread
flour, for dusting
extra virgin olive oil, for
drizzling
Creamy Tzatziki Dip (see
below), to serve

1. Make the pizza dough according to the instructions on page 138, but divide the dough into six portions instead of four. Shape them as instructed, then cover and leave to proof at room temperature for 2–2½ hours.
2. Preheat a large cast-iron or non-stick frying pan (at least 25 cm/10 in) over a medium–high heat.
3. Place one of the dough balls on a lightly floured work surface. Using your fingers, flatten the dough ball into a disc shape, then use a rolling pin to roll the dough into a 23 cm (9 in) round.
4. Brush the frying pan with a little olive oil. Lay the dough round into the hot pan and let it cook for 3–4 minutes until it is golden brown underneath, then flip and cook on the other side for an additional 2–3 minutes. While the flatbread is cooking, roll out the next dough ball so it's ready to add to the pan next. If you have two large frying pans, you can get both going at the same time to make things a little quicker.
5. Once the flatbread is ready, remove it from the pan and wrap it in a clean tea towel to keep it warm. Brush the frying pan with a little more oil and continue with the next flatbread until they're all done.
6. The flatbreads are best served fresh and warm (with the dip below), but you can also make them ahead of time and freeze them. Let them cool completely first, then transfer into a large freezer-safe bag and freeze. You can take them directly from the freezer and toast them either in a toaster, air fryer or oven.

Creamy Tzatziki Dip

**MAKES 600 G
(5¼ OZ/2¼ CUPS)**

1 large cucumber,
coarsely grated
300 g (10½ oz/1¼ cups)
plain full-fat Greek
yoghurt
2 tablespoons extra
virgin olive oil
2 tablespoons freshly
squeezed lemon juice
3 garlic cloves, finely
minced (use more or
less depending on your
preference)
15 g (½ oz/¼ cup) fresh
dill, finely chopped
1 teaspoon flaky sea salt

1. Place the grated cucumber into a piece of muslin (cheesecloth) or a couple of thick paper towels. Wait a few minutes, then squeeze to remove excess moisture from the cucumbers. You will need to squeeze the cloth-wrapped ball of cucumbers very hard multiple times to release as much liquid as possible. Set aside.
2. In a medium bowl, stir together the remaining ingredients, then add the grated cucumber and mix until it is incorporated. Taste for seasoning and add more salt, garlic or lemon juice if you wish. Cover and set aside in the refrigerator for at least a half an hour to let the flavours meld together.
3. This tzatziki can be stored in an airtight container in the fridge for up to 5 days. Drizzle a little extra virgin olive oil over the top before serving with wedges of warm flatbread.

Fougasse with Herby Olive Dipping Oil

A few simple slashes on a ball of pizza dough and you have yourself a stunning fougasse, perfect for tearing, sharing and dunking into some Herby Olive Dipping Oil.

MAKES 1 FOUGASSE TO SERVE 2–3 AS AN APPETIZER OR SIDE

250 g (9 oz) Pizza Dough ball (page 138), fully proofed
plain (all-purpose) or bread flour, for dusting
extra virgin olive oil, for drizzling
flaky sea salt, for sprinkling
herbes de Provence, for scattering (optional)

1. Preheat the oven to 220°C (430°F) and place the oven rack in the lowest position. Line a 23 × 33 cm (9 × 13 in) baking tray with baking parchment.
2. Dust the pizza dough ball with a little flour so it doesn't stick, then gently stretch it into an long oval shape about 25 cm (10 in) long by 10 cm (4 in) wide. Place the dough on the prepared baking tray.
3. Using a pizza cutter, make a 18 cm (7 in) vertical cut down the centre of the oval. Use your fingers to gently expose the cut you've just made by pulling the left and right sides of dough outwards towards the edges of the tray. Now make four evenly spaced diagonal cuts in both the left and right sides of the dough. Position the diagonal cuts to look like veins coming from the stem on a leaf. Spread each section of the dough out towards the edges of the tray to reveal the pattern you've just scored. Arrange the dough as artfully as you can into a leaf shape. The fougasse should be spread out enough that it takes up most of the space on the baking tray.
4. Drizzle the fougasse with olive oil, then sprinkle on some flaky sea salt and some dried herbes de Provence, if using. Bake for 18–22 minutes, or until the bread is turning golden brown and is crispy at the bottom. I always check it after about 16 minutes, and if the base of the bread hasn't crisped up, then I transfer the tray directly to the base of the oven so it can get more direct heat.
5. This bread is best fresh from the oven. Let it cool for a couple of minutes before enjoying warm with the Herby Olive Dipping Oil.

Herby Olive Dipping Oil

MAKES 150 G (5 OZ/SCANT ¾ CUP)

80 ml (2 fl oz/⅓ cup) extra virgin olive oil
1 tablespoon balsamic vinegar
handful of pitted Kalamata or green olives, finely chopped
15 g (½ oz/¼ cup) each of very finely chopped fresh basil leaves and very finely chopped flat-leaf parsley
½ teaspoon dried oregano
1–2 garlic cloves, minced
pinch of dried chilli flakes
½ teaspoon flaky sea salt
freshly ground black pepper

1. In a medium bowl, whisk together the olive oil and balsamic vinegar. Add all the remaining ingredients and stir together until combined.
2. If you make the dipping oil ahead of time, it can be stored in a sealed container in the fridge for up to 3 days. Remove from the fridge at least 30 minutes before using – the oil will solidify in the fridge, so it needs a little time to get back to its liquid state.

Garlic Butter Breadsticks

These breadsticks are so easy to make, and they're such a crowd-pleaser. Be sure to enjoy them warm from the oven with some dips for dunking. If you find yourself with a single spare pizza dough ball, halve this recipe to make a smaller batch of breadsticks.

MAKES 10 BREADSTICKS

fine semolina, for dusting
2 × 250 g (9 oz) Pizza Dough balls (page 138), fully proofed
plain (all-purpose) or bread flour, for dusting
2 tablespoons salted butter
½ teaspoon garlic granules
½ teaspoon dried parsley
Parmesan or vegetarian Italian-style hard cheese, grated (optional)

1. Preheat the oven to 220°C (430°F) and line a large baking tray (33 × 46 cm/13 × 18 in) with non-stick baking parchment. Scatter some fine semolina over the parchment-lined tray.
2. Lightly flour your work surface and transfer one of the pizza dough balls onto it. Stretch the edges of the dough ball out very slightly until it has taken on more of a square shape.
3. Using a dough scraper or pizza cutter, make indentations in the dough ball to demarcate five roughly equal sections across the dough. Cut through the lines you've marked out, then lift each strip of dough, give it a little stretch to lengthen it into a breadstick shape, and place it on the prepared tray. Don't worry if they're not all the same size; just aim for each breadstick to measure 13–18 cm (5–7 in) once stretched out.
4. Repeat this process with the second pizza dough ball, and place the additional breadsticks on the tray, making sure there is a little space between each one.
5. Bake for 12–15 minutes until starting to turn golden brown.
6. While they're baking, melt the butter in a small saucepan over a low heat. Add the garlic granules and dried parsley and stir to combine.
7. Remove the breadsticks from the oven, and use a pastry brush to brush the garlic butter over them while they're still hot. Brush on one coat of butter, let it absorb, then use any remaining garlic butter to brush the breadsticks once more. Scatter a little finely grated Parmesan over the top of the breadsticks if you wish before serving.
8. These breadsticks are best enjoyed fresh from the oven, but they can be brought back to their freshly baked state by warming them up for a few minutes in the oven or air fryer at 190°C (375°F).

TOPPING TIP:

Dip these breadsticks into some Perfect Pizza Sauce (page 161), Fresh Basil Pesto (page 155) or Homemade Ranch Dressing (page 96).

Doughnuts

Frying pizza dough is common practice in Italy. *Pizza fritta, zeppole* ... there are many names for fried pizza dough depending on the region, and the fried dough can be enjoyed with either savoury or sweet toppings. Here, I show you how to turn a couple of pizza dough balls into a batch of warm doughnuts dusted with icing sugar. It is honestly the most dangerous dough hack to have in your repertoire – these doughnuts are so easy to make, and even easier to devour!

MAKES 16 MINI DOUGHNUTS

canola or vegetable oil, for frying
plain (all-purpose) or bread flour, for dusting
2 × 250 g (9 oz) Pizza Dough balls (page 138), fully proofed
2 tablespoons icing (confectioner's) sugar
1 teaspoon ground cinnamon (optional)

1. Pour the oil into a large saucepan or heavy-based cast-iron pot to a depth of 4 cm (1½ in). Place over a medium heat and heat oil until the temperature has reached 175°C (350°F) on a digital thermometer. If you don't have a digital thermometer, you can place a small (2.5 x 2.5 cm/1 x 1 in) cube of bread into the oil to test the temperature. If it fries to a golden brown within 15–25 seconds, the oil is the correct temperature for frying. Frying the doughnuts at the correct temperature is quite crucial. Oil that is too hot can cook the exterior of the doughnut before the interior has cooked, and oil that is too cool may make the doughnuts overly greasy.

2. While the oil is heating, lightly dust your work surface with flour and cut each pizza dough ball into 8 equal pieces of around 30 g (1 oz) each, so you have 16 in total. Use floured hands to shape each of the pieces into mini dough balls. At this point, you can decide if you want to shape them into discs or doughnut rings.

3. For discs, use a rolling pin to roll the dough balls into 7.5 cm (3 in) rounds – or you can just use your hands to flatten/stretch them out. For a ring doughnut poke a hole through the centre of each dough ball with your finger, then twirl the dough around both index fingers until the hole in the middle has stretched out.

4. Depending on the size of your pan, you should be able to fry 4–6 doughnuts at a time. When the oil is ready, add the first batch and fry for 2–3 minutes until golden brown, then flip and fry for 2–3 minutes on the other side. Remove the doughnuts from the hot oil using metal tongs or a wire skimmer, and place them on a plate or tray lined with paper towels to absorb any excess oil. Repeat with the remaining doughnuts.

5. While the doughnuts are still hot, dust them with the sugar. If you're using cinnamon, mix this with the sugar first, then tip into a fine-mesh sieve and dust the doughnuts liberally.

6. Allow the doughnuts to cool for a couple of minutes before enjoying them warm.

TOPPING TIP:

Try spooning some fruit jam or chocolate hazelnut spread onto the doughnuts between each bite for an extra special sweet treat.

Index

A Big Batch of Thank Yous

First and foremost, to my followers on social media - thank you, thank you, thank you! Never in my wildest dreams did I imagine myself writing a cookbook, but YOU are the reason I was given the opportunity to do so. I am eternally grateful for all the ways you've supported me on this journey. Helping you make bread has brought me immeasurable joy, so please never stop sharing photos of your bakes with me!

To my neighbours in Hither Green, South East London, who gave my little micro-bakery, Lace Bakes, a chance. Your unwavering love of bread, pizza dough, cinnamon buns and other baked goodies during lockdown left me with no choice but to practise my newfound breadmaking skills ALL THE TIME. The confidence I gained from that practice set me on the path that has led me to where I am now. Thank you.

To my husband, Chris. Thank you for always believing in me. You knew I should be sharing my recipes and know-how with a wider audience… you called it back in 2020 and I laughed at you and shot the idea down. I promise, I'll listen next time. Special mention for hauling 25-kg (55-lb) bags of bread flour up and down those harrowingly narrow stairs in our London terraced house during the micro-bakery days, how you did it without falling is beyond me.

To my son, Alex. Your love of cooking/cookbooks and your foodie tendencies make me so proud. Never stop tasting new things, because I promise one day you will try something you love even more than my Marinated Tomato & Burrata Pizza. Thank you for your brutally honest taste-testing sessions and for always making me laugh.

To my daughter, Sophie. I'll never forget cuddling with you whilst giving you a sneak peek of the photos that would be in this book. Your carefully curated commentary and appreciation for the most specific details from each shot filled me with such joy. 'Oooh Mummy, that bread looks so fresh and crispy, I want to eat it! Wow, that tomato is so red and juicy, look how red it is Mummy!'. If nobody else appreciates those little details, all the hard work was worth it for you, my girl.

To my parents, Kathy and Dave, through your restaurant ventures you demonstrated that chasing your dreams and being your own boss is worth all the hard work. Thank you for supporting me through the times when this project felt daunting and for celebrating every new step of the journey with me. Though I get embarrassed when you gush about me to random people you meet, I secretly love getting messages on Instagram from strangers who have met you both! To my brother, Austin, thank you for lending your taste-testing services whenever we're both in the same country and for believing in your big sis.

To my in-laws, Ute, Tony, Kathrin and Anna. Thank you for embracing me in your family, for always cheering me on and for the childcare (and a place to stay!) during crazy busy book shoot weeks in London.

To my editor, Issy Gonzalez-Prendergast. Thank you for opening this world up to me, for helping me to fine-tune the concept for *3 Doughs, 60 Recipes* and for guiding me through each step of the process with care, enthusiasm and lots of humour. We did it!

To my agent and fellow bread-lover, Clare Hulton. Thank you for believing in this book and for helping me to navigate the world of book deals and meetings with publishers. Special thanks to Chris Collins for leading me to Clare.

To the design team, Emma Wells and Nikki Dupin from Nic & Lou. You have gone above and beyond to design this joyful and colourful cookbook of my dreams. On one of the shoot days, Emma mentioned they scanned an actual loaf of focaccia to capture the texture of the bubbles for the focaccia chapter opener pages. I mean, if that is not dedication to the job, I do not know what is?

To the copyedit queen, Tara O'Sullivan, thank you for polishing up my words so nicely. I've learned so much from working through your edit notes.

Creating this book was a collaborative effort with the loveliest, most talented creative team. To our brilliant food stylist, Kate Wesson, your level of care, attention to detail and dedication to producing beautiful food is unmatched! Thank you for all your hard work on this project. Kristine Jakobsson, thank you for your laser focus in assisting Kate, for lending your photogenic hands for so many shots and for keeping such a close eye on the ovens to prevent more burnt bread disasters (caused by me!). To our photographer, Steve Joyce, it was a pleasure to work with you and watch you work your magic with the camera. Thank you for ensuring every shot was just right and for energising the team with the best playlists in the studio. To our prop stylist, Jen Kay, thank you for pulling the most perfect props for the shots – your taste is impeccable!

Huge thanks to the entire team at Quadrille UK and particularly to Becky Smedley, Becca Knight and Demeter Scanlon for guiding me through the book launch and all that comes along with it. Thanks to Iman Khabl and the rest of the sales team for your enthusiasm for *3 Doughs, 60 Recipes* and for looking after me during the sales conference. Cheers to Quadrille USA and the team at Chronicle Books for your support stateside.

To my friends, neighbours and extended family – your excitement and encouragement from start to finish of this project has meant the world to me. Special mention to my friend Tanya Baker for being the best hype girl and recipe tester I could ever hope for.

And lastly, to our dog Penny. Thank you for your selfless act of cleaning up all the crumbs and cheese after marathon recipe-testing sessions. What an absolute hero!